SOVIET IMPERIALISM

Russia's Drive Toward

World Domination

By E. DAY CARMAN

PUBLIC AFFAIRS PRESS
Washington, D. C.

ACKNOWLEDGEMENTS

I want to express my appreciation to a number of people for their assistance in connection with this work. First and foremost I am indebted to Professor Paul Mantoux, Co-Director of the Graduate Institute of International Studies in Geneva, Switzerland, for his astute and perspicacious comments and suggestions. Professor Maurice Bourquin of the Institute and the University of Geneva also extended invaluable advice. Mr. Norman Field of the United Nations Library and the staff of that great library were extremely helpful, as was also Mlle. Fayod of the Institute library.

In regard to myriad miscellaneous matters, I owe a great deal of gratitude to the kind assistance of Mme. Alice Goebel, Secretary of the Institute. Miss Nancy Popenoe and Miss Helen Norman also receive my sincere thanks. My good friend Mr. Tennet H. Bagley always came through at the right time; I am indebted to him and, through him, to Mr. Jonathan Daniels, Mr. Lambert Davis, and Fleet Admiral William D. Leahy.

To the following I am grateful for generous courtesies: Messers. Clark Tinch, Peter Geyelin, John Dimmer, William Stearman, Robert Bower, Francis Gross, John Lufkin, Rodney Reilly, Preston Curry, Clearance Moy, William Merrill, Russell Clinkenbeard, the officers and staff of the American Consulate in Geneva, and Mrs. Nita Carman.

For stimulating my interest in international relations, I am grateful to Dr. Leon Ellis, Dr. Claude Buss, Dr. Graham Stuart, and Dr. H. H. Fisher.

Professor William Rappard, Co-Director of the Graduate Institute of International Studies, Professors Hans Wehberg, Paul Guggenheim, and Wilhelm Ropke supplied invaluable information and material in their courses at the Institute.

None can I thank more than my wife Clink Carman, who provided enormous encouragement and indispensable assistance at every stage.

ERNEST DAY CARMAN
Washington, D. C.

3

PREFACE

The scope of this study is Soviet territorial aggrandizement during the ten year period from 1939 to 1949, as such. It does not take into account Soviet Russia's tactics in Poland, Rumania, China, or elsewhere unless those tactics relate directly to the extension of the territorial domain. Moreover, it is not concerned with Soviet occupation policies in Germany, Austria, or Korea. It does, however, take into account those Soviet demands which relate to territory in Iran, Turkey, Tripolitania, Spitsbergen, and other areas. It is essentially an analysis of the concepts and methods underlying Soviet aggrandizement.

Further territorial expansion by the Soviet Union may well result in a third world war. There are of course a variety of other factors which might contribute to a new war, but expansion is the primary one. In this respect, the doctrine of Communism is a cause only in so far as it acts as an agent of Soviet territorial aggrandizement. By way of illustration, there are few who do not abhor the barbaric methods employed within any totalitarian state—Jewish persecutions in Nazi Germany, Protestant persecutions in Fascist Spain, political persecutions in the USSR—but the *casus belli* is latent until such a state seeks to extend its territories at the expense of others.

Studies of history show that the ability of a state to expand is based chiefly on its internal strength and geopolitical factors. Nazi Germany did not necessarily fail because the Allies were right and Hitler's philosophy was wrong. It failed because it had neither the man power, industrial potential, land mass, or over-all strength equal to that of the Allied Powers.

If Britain succeeded in conquering India, the Americans in defeating Mexico, the Spaniards in pillaging the Incas, it was not because their cause was morally right, but because they were materially more advanced. Trotskyites, Falangists, and anarchists present little or no threat to world order not because their doctrines are false or wicked, but because no great state supports their philosophy. The philosophy of Marx is potent primarily because a great state interprets and supports its teachings. As a system of thought it would certainly rank no higher than the teachings of Nietzsche, Schopenhauer, Rousseau, and others, if it were not for the present powerful status of the USSR. Social improvement has been the result not of tyrannical despotisms, but of the efforts of enlightened segments of the population. There has been no advancement by the attempted destruction of one class by another or of one race by another.

The non-Soviet world is, of course, deeply disturbed by the direct territorial expansion by the USSR and indirect expansion through the establishment of Soviet controlled puppet regimes. Conversely, the Russian world is concerned with expansion against the territorial sphere of the USSR. Any eventual change in the present status quo could result in violent conflict. An early prophecy of Stalin may prove correct: "When two giants collide with each other, when this globe is too small for them, they try to measure their strength, they try to solve the vexing question of world hegemony by means of war."[1]

[1] Joseph Stalin, *Problems of Leninism,* (Moscow, 1931), p. 335; from a speech of July 13, 1928.

CONTENTS

CHAPTER 1

THE BACKGROUND OF AGGRANDIZEMENT

"I do not believe that Soviet Russia desires war. What they desire is the fruits of war and the indefinite expansion of their power and doctrines."—Winston Churchill.

The fact that 24,355,500 non-Russian people have been taken into Soviet Russia since 1939 does not seem particularly impressive until it is realized that they constitute a population greater than the total of Canada, Sweden, New Zealand, and Norway. Moreover, the 273,947 square miles of territory acquired at the same time exceeds in area all of France, Belgium, the Netherlands and Portugal combined. Beyond these acquisitions, Soviet influence has probed deep into Central Europe and radiated throughout all of China. Furthermore, along a 2000-mile southern frontier from the western shore of the Black Sea to India, the USSR has maintained a relentless pressure for outlets to the warm seas and decisive influence in the affairs of Asia. Today, whether motivated by a search for security or an expansionist drive, the decisions of the Politburo in international relations affect not only the mute millions of the Soviet Empire but virtually every being on the globe.

The expansion of the Soviet Union has not all been by direct aggression. Both the United States and Great Britain, compelled by the necessities of war, approved beforehand a large part of Russia's territorial gains. However, with these possible exceptions, Soviet policy has been extremely enterprising and presumptuous in any negotiations affecting territory.

Historically the expansionist tendencies of Russia have developed over a long period of time, dating from establishment of the small ninth-century Russian State in the Valley of the Dnieper. Initially, Muscovite expansion seemed to follow the great rivers of Russia—the Volga, Oka, and Dnieper. Later the Tsars extended their territories gradually but forcefully toward Europe in the west and the Ottoman

9

Empire in the southwest. In the east, the Russians experienced much less difficulty in moving their domain slowly across Asia, and to the south they were only partially checked by Persia and Turkestan. In spite of her sprawling empire, however, Russia remained a land-locked nation until the time of Peter the Great. Under his aggressive direction, Russia gained a "window in the west" through the acquisition of Baltic territories, as well as a large portion of what is now European Russia. At the close of the eighteenth century, Catherine II extended Russian dominion yet further and in addition secured the right to send Russian ships through the Black Sea and the Straits onto the sea-lanes of the world.

Russian aggrandizement continued grandly into the nineteenth century.[1] Finland was ceded by Sweden in 1809. Bessarabia became Tsarist territory in 1812. Poland was annexed as an autonomous kingdom following the defeat of Napoleon in 1815. Earlier gains were consolidated in the Caucasus, and the imperial rule was extended to the borders of Afghanistan and Persia. In the Far East, Russia encroached severely on Chinese sovereignty, obtaining from the impotent Manchus not only the right to construct railways across Manchuria, but also full extraterritorial rights to police the land on which these lines ran. Russian influence literally criss-crossed Manchuria, and the Foreign Affairs Office gazed with land-hungry eyes toward South China.

Russian imperialism also crossed the Pacific. In addition to Alaska (which was sold to the United States in 1867), the Tsars claimed land and maintained a fort almost as far south as San Francisco, California.[2] It is not often recalled that Tsarist territorial ambitions in North America contributed to the formulation of the Monroe Doctrine.

By the beginning of World War I, however, Russia's holdings in the Americas had vanished through pressure and sale, and her expansion in the Far East had been dealt a severe blow by a disastrous war with Japan in 1904-05. Nevertheless, the Tsar did not relent in his aspira-

[1] Nineteenth century diplomacy revealed a Russian characteristic quite apparent during the twentieth century. Harold Nicolson (*The Congress of Vienna*, London, 1946, p. 119) writes that during 1815 "Russian generals and diplomats, having convinced themselves that Russian arms alone had liberated Europe from an odious tyranny . . . began on every occasion and in every country to indulge in self-assertiveness and intrigue. . . . At the same time from the remotest corners of Europe, Asia, Africa, and even America reports began to pour in in regarding the presence of mysterious Russian agents and the activities of energetic and overbearing Russian diplomatists. Such reports were too numerous, too frequent, and withall, too consistent to be ignored."

[2] The Russians maintained Fort Ross approximately 60 miles north of San Francisco until the early 1840's.

tions for more land. Russia's participation in World War I was accompanied by extensive territorial demands. In his study *Russia and Postwar Europe,* David J. Dallin states:

"On the basis of the diplomatic (mostly secret) documents of 1914-1917 that have so far been made public, and on the basis of public statements of responsible political figures of that period the Russian plan of territorial acquisition can be stated in these terms:

" 'All Polish territories were to be unified within the framework of the Russian Empire. This meant the addition to the former Polish territories in Russia of the Polish provinces in Austria (so-called Western Galicia) and the Polish provinces in Germany (the Pozan and Pomorze regions). The Russian frontier in the west would have coincided roughly with the Polish frontiers of 1919-1939. The Russian frontier in the Polish north would have touched the Baltic Sea somewhere near Danzig-Stettin.

" 'East Prussia was to be annexed to Russia. Thus all the territories lying east of the Vistula would have been brought within the borders of the Russian Empire.

" 'Eastern Galicia, populated mainly by Ukranians, was to be transferred from Austrian to Russian dominion. Together with this province, the northern section of Bucovina was to become a Russian possession, while southern Bucovina was to be joined to Rumania.

" 'The northeastern provinces of Hungary, which had a considerable Slavonic minority, were to be ceded to Russia. . . .

" 'Turkey was to be ousted from Europe, while Russia was to receive . . . Constantinople.

" 'In Asia, some of the Turkish territories bordering on Transcaucasia were to be ceded to Russia.' "

The final result, it will be remembered, was quite different. Principally because of complete war exhaution, Russia succumbed to revolution. The Bolsheviks subsequently seized control from the original revolutionaries and shortly thereafter concluded a separate peace with the Central Powers. The separate peace was the Treaty of Brest-Litovsk, certainly one of the most grasping, rapacious treaties of modern times. This treaty, together with its annexes and supplements, forced Russia to relinquish to Germany and Austria-Hungary the territories of Russian Poland, Lithuania, Courland, Livonia, Estonia, and the Islands of the Moon Sound. To Turkey she was forced to cede Kars and Ardahan. Furthermore, she was compelled to recognize the independence of the Ukraine and to shoulder reparation payments totalling six billion marks, of which 120 million gold rubles were actually paid before the collapse of the Central Powers.[3] In all, the Russian Government of the Bolsheviks lost an estimated 1,267,000 square miles of territory with over 62,000,000 people, or one-fourth of Russia's total area and 44% of her population—including one-third of her agricultural land, 85% of her beet-sugar land, 89% of her coal mines, 73% of her iron, 54% of her industry and 27% of her state income.[4]

Since the Tsar's plans for the spoils of victory were hardly less pretentious than those of the Kaiser, it was obvious that both were playing for large territorial stakes.

When, subsequently, the Bolsheviks took power in the midst of near chaos, the acceptance of the extortionist Treaty of Brest-Litovsk was considered by Lenin as the necessary "breathing spell" that enabled the proletarian dictatorship to survive. There is little doubt that if Lenin's government had not accepted the humiliating peace the German armies would have continued their advance through Petrograd, Moscow, and most of Western Russia. Without their dearly purchased period of partial peace, the Bolsheviks probably would have been eliminated either by the Germans or by counter-revolutionary forces within Russia. As events have shown, the Soviet Government miraculously survived the brutal horrors of revolution, foreign intervention, and Bolshevik impetuousness and incompetence. In retrospect, there were a multitude of events which slightly changed would have altered profoundly the course of world history.

During the era of Bolshevik turmoil which followed the armistice of November, 1918, Russia's territorial status was in almost constant flux. For a while, following Brest-Litovsk, the Ukraine operated as an independent government with strong German support. Armenia, Georgia, and Azerbaijan also exercised some characteristics of sovereign states. Rumania succeeded in gaining control of Bessarabia. Turkey, although a Central Power, appropriated the bordering areas of Kars and Ardahan. Persia was said to have expressed grand designs for expansion into the Baku region.[5] Finland, Poland, Estonia, Latvia, and

[3] J. W. Wheeler-Bennett, "From Brest-Litovsk to Brest-Litovsk", *Foreign Affairs*, January 1940.

[4] James Bunyan and H. H. Fisher, *The Bolshevik Revolution 1917–1918*, (Stanford University 1934), pp. 523-4. Also Wheeler-Bennett *The Treaty of Brest-Litovsk, and Germany's Eastern Policy* (Oxford 1939), pp. 10-11.

[5] According to an article in the *Soviet News*, March 16, 1946, Iran demanded at the end of World War I almost half the Caucasus including the whole of Azerbaijan, Armenia, part of Daghestan—in all some 200,000 square miles. This alleged request was in the form of a memorandum by the Iranian Government in 1919 but was never examined by the Peace Conference, the article claimed.

Lithuania were recognized as independent. In the Far East, Japan for a considerable length of time occupied the Maritime Provinces and areas as far west as Lake Baikal. From various places and all directions, counter-revolutionary forces operated against the Bolshevik Government, generally with confused, partially effective material and financial support from certain Allied Powers. It is not surprising that as this era passed into one of contrasting calm, the Soviet Government appeared and doubtless was very anxious for world peace—certainly until such a time as the Proletarian State would have the power to assert its ideology in a bourgeois world more effectively. The era of turmoil was nevertheless of some value. Certain techniques and ideas for the extension of territory were developed which appeared in later Soviet dealings.

It is interesting to note that the Bolsheviks during the first years of their regime apparently awaited the so-called imperialist war to be converted into a series of civil wars which in turn would be the prelude to world revolution.[6] Evidently expecting that in Europe these civil wars would result in a number of new proletarian states, the first Soviet Constitution of 1918, provided for territorial expansion through voluntary adhesion. Russia, and later the Soviet Union, was to be a federation of all countries in which the proletariat had overthrown the landlords and capitalists. In that it was the first nation seized by the proletariat, Russia would serve both as the arsenal of world revolution and as the magnet to states falling away from capitalism. As Stalin put it: "For the slogan 'the United States of Europe', we will substitute the slogan 'the federation of soviet republics of advanced countries and colonies which have fallen or are falling away from the imperialist system of economy.' "[7]

On this basis, Russia and three Russian territories constructed as Soviet republics (Ukrainia, Byelorussia, and Transcaucasia), signed a Treaty of Union on December 30, 1922. They were joined by two more of these so-called republics, the Turkmen and Uzbek, in 1925, and by the Tajik Soviet Republic a short time later. In 1936, the Kazakh and Kirghiz areas were designated by the Politburo as Soviet Republics, and the Transcaucasian Soviet Republic was dissolved into Georgia, Armenia, and Azerbaijan. To these eleven were added five new republics during the course of World War II: Estonian, Latvian, Lithuanian, Karelo-Finnish, and Moldavian.

The foundation of the Soviet republican system is set forth in Article 123 of the 1936 Constitution:

[6] Stalin, *Problems of Leninism*, (Moscow, 1945), p. 54.
[7] Stalin, *Problems of Leninism*, (Moscow, 1931), pp. 337-8.

"Equality of rights of citizens of the USSR, irrespective of their nationality or race, in all spheres of economic, state, cultural, social and political life, is an indefeasible law.

"Any direct or indirect restriction of the rights of, or, conversely, any establishment of direct or indirect privileges for, citizens on account of their race or nationality, as well as any advocacy of racial or national exclusiveness or hatred and contempt, is punishable by law."

Both the federal structure of the USSR and the Soviet nationality policy are based on this premise. If one can set aside the class persecution generated in Communist doctrine, it is on its face value an ideal guarantee. Upon it is established the geographic and administrative structure of the multinational Soviet Union. The 16 republics, 16 autonomous republics, 9 autonomous regions, and 10 national districts are organized according to the national characteristics and cultural achievement of their composite groups and peoples. However, with the possible exception of freedom from dire want, freedom in these areas is doubtless strictly limited; nevertheless, the system has helped to develop cultural and political identity and in some degree prevented racial antagonisms and genocide. There is, however, considerable evidence that the Soviet Union has violated this basic guarantee on several occasions (see Chapter XVI).

The nationality arrangement carries through to the bicameral legislative branch of government. The Supreme Soviet is elected by proportional representation of one deputy for each 300,000 population. The second chamber, the Soviet of Nationalities, is elected on the basis of so many deputies for a certain type unit in the federal structure— for instance, twenty-five for a Union Republic, and five for an Autonomous Region. Theoretically at least, all ethnic groups are fairly represented in the Supreme Soviet.

In this federal structure one would suppose that the highest federal unit would be a Soviet Socialist Republic. It is not. In spite of the fact that a Union Republic is presented in the constitution as an independent nation-state with certain sovereign rights including the right to secede, the Autonomous Republics, apparently a type of secondary subdivision, sometimes enjoy higher status. On November 25, 1936, Stalin rejected a proposal that Autonomous Republics be raised to the status of Union Republics upon attaining a certain level of economic and cultural development, arguing as follows:

"This would not be a Marxist, not a Leninist approach. The Tatar Republic, for example, remains an Autonomous Republic, while the Kazakh Republic is to become a Union Republic; but this does not mean that from the standpoint of culture and economic development the Kazakh Republic is on a higher level than the Tatar Republic. The very opposite is the case. The same can be said, for example of the Volga-German Autonomous Republic[8] and the Kirghiz Union Republic, of which the former is on a higher cultural and economic level than the latter, although it remains an Autonomous Republic. What are the grounds for transferring Autonomous Republics to the category of Union Republics? There are three such grounds.

"First, the republic concerned must be a border republic, not surrounded on all sides by USSR territory. Why? Because since the Union Republics have a right to secede from the USSR, a republic, on becoming a Union Republic, must be in a position logically and actually to raise the question of secession from the USSR. And this question can be raised only by a republic which, say, borders on some foreign State, and consequently is not surrounded on all sides by USSR territory. Of course, none of our republics would actually raise the question of seceding from the USSR. But since the right to secede from the USSR is reserved to Union Republics, it must be so arranged that this right does not become a meaningless scrap of paper . . .

"Secondly, the nationality which gives its name to a given Soviet republic must constitute a more or less compact majority within that republic. Take the Crimean Autonomous Republic,[9] for example. It is a border republic, but the Crimean Tartars do not constitute the majority in that republic; on the contrary, they are a minority. Consequently, it would be wrong and illogical to transfer the Crimean Republic to the category of Union Republic.

"Thirdly, the republics must not have too small a population; it should have a population of, say, not less by more than a million, at least. Why? Because it would be wrong to assume that a small Soviet republic with a very small population and a small army could hope to maintain its existence as an independent State. There can hardly be any doubt that the imperialist beasts of prey would soon lay hands on it."[10]

This is an important explanation to remember, for upon it derives a basic expansionist technique of the USSR, a useful expedient for both

[8] The Volga-German Autonomous Republic was abolished in 1941, and its population presumably scattered over large parts of the Soviet Far East. All cities and towns, all geographic names of German origin were changed to Russian. The same fate befell certain other entities in the USSR.

[9] The Crimean Autonomous Republic was also abolished during World War II.

[10] Requoted from Frederick L. Schuman, *Soviet Politics At Home and Abroad*, (New York, 1948), pp. 311-12.

Communism and Russianism. The technique will be observed more fully as this study progresses.

Another interesting development of the period prior to 1939—and also institutionalized later as an instrument of expansion—occurred during December of 1918. Perhaps believing the world revolution at hand, the Bolsheviks formed Communist puppet governments on Russian territory for Estonia, Latvia, and Lithuania. The Bolsheviks immediately negotiated treaties of military assistance with these allegedly legal governments by which the Red Army was invited to enter the territory of the state in question and establish the puppet regime as the legal government. The Leningrad *Izvestiya* of December 25, 1918, stated that the Baltic Sea had to become a "Sea of Soviet Revolution", that the independent Baltic States stood in the way of Soviet Russia to Western Europe and had to be eliminated, if necessary by force.[11]

In addition to the Baltic experiment, a Communist government existed on southern Finnish soil until 1919. There were two other Soviet governments the same year. In Hungary, Soviet rule was proclaimed on March 21, 1919. It endured for a few months before being crushed by Rumanian invaders and forces under Admiral Horthy. A much shorter Soviet regime reigned in Bavaria during the last weeks of April, 1919, but it too was quickly suppressed.

For one reason or another, the early Communist adventures failed. Contrary to Bolshevik expectations, the Versailles conference did not collapse nor did Europe explode in social revolution. Brief victories in Hungary and Bavaria were abortive, and early Communist attempts at puppet governments in exile were frustrated. Peace treaties with bordering states soon followed. The Narkomindel (Russian Foreign Office) had sensed the changed conditions, and begun to act accordingly.

The peace treaties signed by the USSR with the Baltic countries in February 1920 were based on the principle of national self determination, a principle proclaimed by the Bolsheviks as early as November 15, 1917. The Tsarist annexationist treaties of the eighteenth century were expressly denounced by the Soviets in the text of the treaties and Baltic independence was recognized forever. The cornerstone of future relations was to be strict Soviet non-interference in Baltic domestic affairs. Simultaneously the puppet governments founded by the USSR in 1918 were quietly dissolved.

Postwar events in Finland followed a similar line. A treaty of the same general character was signed October 14, 1920.

[11] Alfred Bilmanis, *Baltic States and World Peace and Security Organization,* (Washington, D. C., 1945), pp. 15-16.

The situation in Poland was somewhat different. The Soviet Union in 1920 was faced with an imperialistic, land-grabbing neighbor which resorted to warfare to achieve its ends. Historical evidence indicates that Poland instigated this war solely to extend the disputed Russo-Polish border far into the interior of Russia. Striving to avoid hostilities, the Soviet Government actually offered the Poles a boundary considerably east of the 1921-1939 frontier, but the Poles refused. During the war that followed, after advancing as far as Kiev, the Poles shortly found themselves defending their own capital at Warsaw. It was at this juncture that the Bolsheviks made use of a Communist-dominated puppet government once more. This Bolshevik group advanced along with the Red Army and proclaimed itself the legal government of all Poland. The move, however, was premature. With outside assistance the Poles managed to drive the Red Army slowly back and with it the Communist puppet regime. Largely because of exhaustion, the Moscow Government was compelled to sign the Treaty of Riga on March 18, 1921, an agreement establishing the 1921-1939 boundaries which the United States and most European governments refused to recognize until 1923.

In the Caucasus, Georgia, Armenia, and Azerbaijan proclaimed their independence after 1917. The Azerbaijan Government was short-lived, but the Armenian and Georgian Governments continued to exist into the early 1920's. They were finally brought under Moscow control by the Red Army and accompanying puppet Soviet regimes. One authority has suggested that this early technique has not changed, but its increased effectiveness lies in the fact that the strength of the Red Army has changed.[12]

Soviet action in the Far East was concerned until 1922 with suppressing counter revolts (Admiral Kolchak and the Czech Legions primarily), opposing Allied—principally Japanese—occupation of Siberia, and, until 1925, ousting a prolonged Japanese occupation of northern Sakhalin Island. In spite of these rather formidable tasks, the USSR was nevertheless able to carry on an active foreign policy with its Far Eastern neighbors.

In China, collaboration between the Nationalist revolutionaries of Sun Yat-sen and the Communists was particularly close during the early 1920's. At the same time, the Bolsheviks pursued a strong policy toward Outer Mongolia. Counter-revolutionary forces under Baron Ungern-Sternberg had seized control of this country during 1920. The

<hr />

12 W. Gurian, "Permanent Features of Soviet Foreign Policy," *The Year Book of World Affairs 1947,* (London, 1947), pp. 33-34.

Baron's forces were eventually defeated by a combination of both Red Army and Mongolian troops. Shortly thereafter a treaty was concluded between the Soviet Union and the temporary Revolutionary Mongol Government (not at that time a "People's Republic"). The most important clause of this 1921 treaty enjoined each government not to allow on the other's territory the transportation of arms, the formation of enemy groups, or the recruiting or transit of troops hostile to the other contracting party. Following the treaty, the Soviet Government supplied the Mongols with a number of technical advisors and specialists who assisted in the purported modernization of the republic.

The somewhat dubious character of the treaty and a duplicious taint in Soviet intentions is apparent in Part Four of a joint statement issued a short time later by Sun Yat-sen and the Soviet envoy to China, A. A. Joffe. "Mr. Joffe has categorically declared to Dr. Sun," it said, "that it is not and never has been the intention or purpose of the present Russian Government to pursue an imperialistic policy in Outer Mongolia or to cause it to secede from China."[13]

In a review of the period between 1921 and 1939, it is interesting to note that the USSR never once complained about the frontiers of Poland, Finland, Turkey, or Iran; nor did it assert itself against the independence of the Baltic States. The only Kremlin protest was directed at Rumania's incorporation of Bessarabia. The Soviet Union neither recognized Rumanian ownership of Bessarabia nor had much to do with the Bucharest regime prior to June 1940, when the Red Army took possession of the disputed area.

The USSR not only respected the territorial integrity of bordering governments, but on July 4, 1933, went one step further. It guaranteed the borders of these states against aggression. The instrument of this guarantee was the Convention for the Definition of Aggression signed by the USSR, Czechoslovakia, Lithuania, Turkey, Yugoslavia, and later by Estonia, Latvia, Finland, Poland, Afghanistan, and Iran. The author of the Convention was Maxim Litvinov, at that time Foreign Affairs Commissar of the Soviet Union.

Article 2 of this document stated that an aggressor would be considered to be that state which first took any of the following actions:

"Declaration of war upon another state."

"Invasion by its armed forces, with or without declaration of war, of the territory of another state."

"Attack by its land, naval, or air forces, with or without a declara-

---

[13] Owen Lattimore, "The Outer Mongolian Horizon," *Foreign Affairs*, July 1946.

tion of war, on the territory, vessels, or aircraft of another state. . . ."

"Naval blockade of the coast or ports of another state."

"Support to armed bands formed on its territory which have invaded another state. . . ."

Even more specific was the annex to the Convention. It stated that no acts of aggression could be justified by "The internal condition of a state, for example: its political, economic, or social structure, alleged defects in its administration, disturbances due to strikes, revolutions, counter-revolutions, or civil war. . . ."

Yet within eight years the Soviet Union had, according to its own definition of aggression, violated this convention in Estonia, Latvia, Lithuania, Poland, Finland, and Iran—all signatories of the 1933 pact.

CHAPTER 2

THE NAZI-SOVIET PACT AND POLAND

"If you like a foreign province and you have enough force, take it immediately. As soon as you have done that you will always find enough lawyers who will prove that you were entitled to the occupied territory."—Frederick II of Prussia.

Soviet Russia demanded and obtained a high price for her services as an ally in 1939. For the Anglo-French grouping of powers this price was apparently too high and the conflicting interests too many. But for Nazi Germany, once its plan of conquest had been definitely decided upon, any wild promise of the moment was a necessary expedient. Under such circumstances, the advantages accruing to Soviet Russia were many. First and foremost, by signing a neutrality pact with Hitler, the Kremlin gained time to prepare defenses for an eventual attack by some hostile power (Soviet writers have since maintained that this power was Germany). Next, the Soviet Union was given a virtually free hand in eastern Europe by the Nazis. As a final *quid pro quo,* Russia received a generous slice of a then soon to be dismembered Poland.

Dated August 23, 1939, the Treaty of Nonaggression was negotiated with amazing rapidity. It was as if the two totalitarian states had suddenly realized that each was indispensable to the other, although in fact both had been cautiously maneuvering toward the possibility of an alliance for the previous five months. According to the German time table, Poland was to be attacked on the first day of September 1939. Consequently, there was a rush on the part of the Germans to conclude this pact prior to that date. Hitler prodded Stalin in a telegram on August 20th, emphasizing that "The tension between Germany and Poland has become intolerable. Polish demeanor toward a great power is such that a crisis may arise any day."[1]

[1] Reich Foreign Minister to German Ambassador in the Soviet Union, August 20, 1939. *Documents from the Archives of the German Foreign Office, Nazi-Soviet Relations 1939-1941,* Department of State, (Washington, D. C., 1948), pp. 66-7.

The Russians were anxious to insure their neutrality but nevertheless desired additional time to prepare for final negotiations with the Nazis. However, under heavy pressure, they considered it wise to reply immediately. Stalin therefore wired Hitler on August 21 that the Soviet Union would be amenable to final treaty talks with Herr von Ribbentrop, the German Foreign Minister, in Moscow on August 23.[2]

Actually, two days before (on August 21), Molotov had presented Schulenburg, the German Ambassador in Moscow, with a preliminary draft of a proposed nonaggression pact. The text of the draft was generally the same as the final treaty, but affixed to it was a revealing postscript: "The present pact shall be valid only if a special protocol is signed simultaneously covering the points in which the High Contracting Parties are interested in the field of foreign policy. The protocol shall be an integral part of the pact."[3]

This special protocol, known as the "Secret Additional Protocol", stated: "On the occasion of the signature of the Nonaggression Pact between the German Reich and the Union of Soviet Socialist Republics, the undersigned plenipotentiaries of each of the two parties discussed in strictly confidential conversations the question of the boundary of their respective spheres of influence in Eastern Europe. These conversations led to the following conclusions:

"1. In the event of a territorial and political rearrangement in the areas belonging to the Baltic States (Finland, Estonia, Latvia, and Lithuania), the northern boundary of Lithuania shall represent the boundary of the spheres of influence of Germany and the USSR. In this connection the interest of Lithuania in the Vilna area is recognized by each party.

"2. In the event of a territorial and political rearrangement of the areas belonging to the Polish state the spheres of influence of Germany and the USSR shall be bounded approximately by the line of the rivers Narew, Vistula, and San.

"The question of whether the interests of both parties make desirable the maintenance of an independent Polish state and how such a state should be bounded can only be definitely determined in the course of further political developments.

"In any event both Governments will resolve this question by means of a friendly agreement.

"3. With regard to Southeastern Europe attention is called by the Soviet side to its interest in Bessarabia. The German side declares its complete political disinterestedness in these areas.

2 *Documents, op. cit.*, p. 69.   3 *Ibid.*, p. 65-6.

"4. This protocol shall be treated by both parties as strictly secret."[4]

This then was the definitive reward to the USSR for signing a non-aggression agreement with Germany. So anxious was Hitler to conquer Poland, and to insure a neutral Russia in case of war with Britain and France, that he had promised the Kremlin a free hand in the Baltic regions north of Lithuania, Bessarabia in the Balkan area, as well as a generous piece of Poland. Seldom has so much been offered for a benevolent neutrality. Here was an opportunity, eagerly seized by the Kremlin, to regain a large part of the areas lost in World War I. Here too was a chance to gain ground for strategic defense: defense against Germany should the Fuhrer go back on his promises; defense against any other Power or grouping of Powers which might some day endanger the land of Socialism. But in another sense, here was a grand base for offense—an offense that would not only make the USSR the predominant power of the Baltic, but give needed ice-free ports to the growing Red Fleet, provide a stronger voice in Eastern Europe, establish a nearer approach to the Straits, and expand Communism. Small wonder that Russia grasped the opportunity! Britain and France would never have given as much in a thousand years. And all for doing nothing, for remaining neutral, for signing a nonaggression pact with Nazi Germany.

In the text of the Nonaggression Pact itself, there was nothing new. The same type of instrument had been negotiated many times during the Litvinov era. Unlike most earlier agreements, however, it did not contain a clause providing for abrogation or denunciation in case one of the signatories was drawn into war under conditions which might qualify that country as an aggressor. The reason why it did not was clear. The Secret Protocol left no doubt as to Hitler's intentions, and Soviet Russia expected to share in the profits of an aggressive war. Soviet public explanations remained necessarily very weak. In an annoyed tone Molotov remarked shortly thereafter that "There are wiseacres who construe from the pact more than is written in it. For this purpose, all kinds of conjectures and hints are mooted about in order to cast doubt on the pact in one country or another. But all this merely speaks for the hopeless impotence of the enemies of the pact!"[5]

Molotov's last sentence was subsequently to ring all too true.

World War II began a few days after the signing of the pact, and the outcome looked so encouraging to Germany within forty-eight

[4] *Documents, op. cit.*, p. 78.

[5] Molotov's speech at the fourth special session of the Supreme Soviet of the USSR, August 31, 1939.

hours after attacking Poland that Ribbentrop dispatched a revealing
telegram to Schulenburg in Moscow: "We definitely expect to have
beaten the Polish Army decisively in a few weeks. We would then keep
the area that was established as German sphere of interest at Moscow
under military occupation. We would naturally, however, for military
reasons, also have to proceed further against such Polish military forces
as are at that time located in the Polish area belonging to the Russian
sphere of interest. Please discuss this at once with Molotov and see if
the Soviet Union does not consider it desirable for Russian forces to
move at the proper time against Polish forces in the Russian sphere of
interest and, for their part, to occupy this territory. In our estimation
this would be not only a relief for us, but also, in the sense of the Moscow agreements, in the Soviet interest as well." [6]

Moscow's reply agreed it would be absolutely necessary to start concrete action at a suitable time, but debated as to whether that time had
arrived. "It is possible that we are mistaken," admitted the Kremlin,
"but it seems to us that through excessive haste we might injure our
cause and promote unity among our opponents." [7]

No further information was immediately forthcoming from Moscow.
On September 8, however, Molotov phoned Schulenburg with the following message: "I have received your communication regarding the
entry of German troops into Warsaw. Please convey my congratulations
and greetings to the German Reich Government." [8] A few hours later,
Molotov informed Schulenburg that Soviet military action would take
place within the next few days.

It was obvious that the rapid German advance had surprised the
Soviet leaders. Even after the Nazis had been notified of Russian military plans the Red Army was a week away from effective mobilization.

Meanwhile the German Army continued to advance across Poland.
Molotov confessed to Schulenburg on September 9 his complete surprise and stated that "everything possible was being done to expedite
matters." He then revealed that the Soviet Government intended to
take the occasion of the German advance to declare that Poland was
falling apart and it was therefore necessary for his government to come
to the aid of the Ukrainians and White Russians "threatened" by Ger-

---

[6] Ribbentrop to Schulenburg, September 3, 1939, *Documents, op. cit.,* p. 86. Ribbentrop evidently attached great importance to this telegram for prefixing it were the
words "Very Urgent! Exclusively for Ambassador. Strictly Secret! For Chief of Mission or his representative personally. Top Secret! To be decoded by himself. Strict-
est Secrecy!"

[7] Schulenburg to Foreign Office, September 5, 1939, *Documents, op. cit.,* p. 87.

[8] *Ibid.,* September 8, 1939, p. 89.

many. This argument was designed to make Russian intervention sound plausible to the masses and at the same time to avoid giving the Soviet Union the appearance of an aggressor. The German Foreign Office, upon hearing Molotov's reasoning, naturally opposed the Soviet idea as throwing suspicion on German intentions. Ribbentrop then suggested a joint communiqué, but the Soviet Government demurred with a modification of its original proposal.

According to Molotov, the USSR now intended to rationalize its actions as follows: "the Polish State had collapsed and no longer existed; therefore, all agreements concluded with Poland were void; third powers might try to profit by the chaos which had arisen; the Soviet Union considered itself obliged to intervene to protect its Ukrainian and White Russian brothers and make it possible for these unfortunate people to work in peace."[9] Molotov went on to say that when the Red Army had crossed the border, on the morning of September 17, the Soviet Government intended to publicize its reasoning by press and radio. At the same time, Molotov would communicate the Kremlin attitude to the Polish Ambassador in an official note.

On September 17, true to his word, Molotov gave a classic explanation of the Soviet invasion of Poland: "One cannot expect the Soviet Government to remain indifferent to the fate of our kindred Ukrainians and White Russians inhabiting Poland whose status heretofore was that of nations without any rights and who are at present subjected to the will of chance. The Soviet Government deems it its sacred duty to extend a helping hand to our brother Ukrainians and brother White Russians who live in Poland."[10]

The note to the unbelieving Polish Ambassador was couched in the same vein. "The Polish state," it said, "and its government have, in fact, ceased to exist. Therefore the agreements concluded between the USSR and Poland have ceased to operate." The brother Ukrainians and brother White Russians who live in Poland "are at the mercy of fate . . . under these circumstances, the Soviet Government has directed the High Command of the Red Army to order the troops to cross the frontier and to take under their protection the life and property of the population of Western White Russia."

This method of reasoning had as its basis the multinational character of the Soviet Union. It was much the same as the professed Nazi interest in the foreign-situated *Volksdeutsche,* but considerably more promising—the USSR could multiply the idea by the considerable

---

[9] Schulenburg to Foreign Office, September 15, 1939, *Documents, op. cit.,* p. 95.
[10] *New York Times,* September 18, 1939.

number of nationalities in the Union. It is a powerful technique; with each new territorial addition there accrue new nationality additions. The Soviet nationalities can therefore be utilized in much the same manner as an atomic chain reaction if so ignited by the Politburo.

On September 18, the day following the Russian attack, Germany and the USSR drafted a joint communiqué explaining their actions. This had been done with some difficulty since Stalin had felt that an original German draft was not phrased with sufficient delicacy. He personally rewrote the communiqué which was then broadcast with the full consent of the German Government. It stated:

"In order to avoid all kinds of unfounded rumors concerning the respective aims of the German and Soviet forces which are operating in Poland, the Government of the German Reich and the Government of the USSR declare that the operations of these forces do not involve any aims which are contrary to the interests of Germany and of the Soviet Union, or to the spirit or the letter of the Nonaggression Pact concluded between Germany and the USSR. On the contrary, the aim of these forces is to restore peace and order in Poland, which had been destroyed by the collapse of the Polish State, and to help the Polish population to reconstruct the conditions of its political existence."[11]

If the joint communiqué meant that the USSR and Germany were going to reconstruct the Polish State as a political entity, then both Powers had changed their original intentions within forty-eight hours. Molotov hinted to Schulenburg on September 20 that the initial inclinations of the Soviet Government to permit the existence of a residual Poland had given way to a new desire to partition Poland along the Pisa-Narew-Vistula-San Line. The German Government immediately expressed agreement with this idea. Shortly thereafter, Stalin told Schulenburg that in the final settlement of the Polish question anything which in the future might cause friction between the Soviet Union and Germany must be avoided. From this point of view, he considered it wrong to leave an independent Polish rump state. Stalin proposed that from the territory to the east of the demarcation line, all the province of Lublin and that portion of the province of Warsaw which extended to the Bug should be added to the German share. In return, Germany would waive its claim to Lithuania. If the Germans consented, said Stalin, the Soviet Union would immediately take up the solution of the problem of the Baltic countries in accordance with the Protocol of August 23, and would expect the "unstinting" support of the German Government. Stalin expressly indicated Estonia,

11 *Documents, op. cit.,* p. 100.

Latvia, and Lithuania as countries in need of "solution." He did not mention Finland.[12]

In order to handle all problems arising from the Protocol, Ribbentrop personally flew to Moscow on September 27, 1939. He was feted royally. The atmosphere in Moscow was one of jubilance and triumph. One report has it that Ribbentrop even learned a few verses of Georgian poetry which he recited to a pleased Stalin shortly after arriving. And as a mark of especial respect, the Soviet radio refrained for an entire day from broadcasting Communist propaganda in German.[13]

The German-Soviet Boundary and Friendship Treaty was the first result of the parley, and it adhered closely to Stalin's proposals of September 25. The new frontier followed the rivers Bug, Pisa, and San at a distance of about eighty or so miles to the east of Warsaw. The new arrangement was documented in a Secret Supplementary Protocol which amended the previous Secret Protocol of August 23. In the words of the agreement itself, "the Lithuanian State falls to the sphere of influence of the USSR, while, on the other hand, the province of Lublin and parts of the province of Warsaw fall to the sphere of influence of Germany."[14] In addition, a small strip of southwestern Lithuania was reserved for Germany. Both parties also agreed to tolerate no Polish action in their territories which would affect the territories of the other party and to "suppress all beginnings of such agitation and inform each other concerning suitable measures for this purpose."

Lastly, Article III of the Treaty sanctioned measures for full political incorporation: "The necessary reorganization of public administration will be effected in the areas west of the line specified by the Government of the German Reich, and in the areas east of this line by the Government of the USSR."

This article was of particular importance to the Russians. Only three weeks later, on October 22, a typical Communist election was held in the Polish provinces seized by Russia. The purpose was to elect representatives to "People's Assemblies." As usual, better than ninety percent of the eligible voters cast their ballots, and the figures showed that better than ninety percent of the votes had gone to the candidates of various Communist-approved organizations. Within a matter of days, the newly elected People's Assembly of the Western Ukraine in turn passed a resolution requesting that its territory be annexed to the Soviet

[12] Schulenburg to Foreign Office, September 25, 1939, *Documents, op. cit.*, pp. 102-03.

[13] Dallin, *Soviet Russia's Foreign Policy 1939-1942* (New Haven, 1942), pp. 76-77.

[14] *Documents, op. cit.*, September 28, 1939, pp. 105-7.

Union, and that all large industries, banks, and land be confiscated by the State. The same process occurred in White Russia. The Supreme Soviet of the USSR wasted no time in recommending that the requests be granted and that the former eastern provinces of Poland be formally affixed to the Soviet Union.

Thus the USSR gained 76,500 miles of territory and a population of 12,800,000, of whom approximately seven million were "kindred" Ukrainians, and some three million were "brother" White Russians. The balance consisted of about a million Poles and a million Jews. In Soviet eyes the legality of the transaction was beyond question. The Socialist Motherland had extended the Communist principle to more non-Soviet people in a month than it had in all of its previous twenty years history. For the records at least, ninety percent of them had expressed their gratitude at the polls. From then on, the future of Eastern Poland was to be solely a matter of internal Soviet politics.

Strategically, the new land was not vitally important. The area provided depth, but no natural frontier barriers. Moreover, the German-controlled, wedge-shaped Suwalki district menaced Soviet defense plans in the west. Offensively, however, the new borders with Lithuania were of immediate value, and those with the Czechoslovak Carpathian Ukraine were to prove most helpful at the end of World War II.

In a little more than a month, the alliance with Nazi Germany had conclusively demonstrated its worth. But the dividends had just begun. There was much more to come.

CHAPTER 3

THE NAZI-SOVIET PACT AND THE BALTIC STATES

"We stand for an exact and honest fulfillment of agreement signed by us on a basis of mutuality and declare that foolish prattle of the Sovietization of the Baltic States is of use merely to our common enemies."—Molotov, 1940.

The rapid advance of the German Army in Poland prompted the Politburo to lose no time in taking advantage of a promising situation in the Baltic. On the same day that the Red Army crossed the Polish frontier, Moscow press releases insinuated that Estonia was acting in an unfriendly manner toward the USSR. Karl Selter, the Estonian Foreign Minister, was shortly summoned to Moscow for ostensible "trade negotiations" with the Soviet Government. The "trade", however, was not what Selter had envisioned and the alarmed Foreign Minister hastily returned to the Estonian capital, Tallinn, only two days later. His alarm was well-founded. That very day, September 25, Russian aircraft carried on extensive flights over Estonian territory and new detachments of the Red Army moved up to the Estonian border. Rossing, the German Military Attaché in Estonia, cabled Berlin that the Estonian Chief of Staff had informed him of a Moscow ultimatum for a Soviet-Estonian alliance. Since foreign aid appeared unlikely, Rossing continued, the Estonian General Staff had reluctantly advised Selter to accept the Russian demands—which included a naval base at Baltishport and an air base on the Estonian Islands.[1]

Estonia was in fact helpless. Her only possible allies, Latvia and Lithuania, were at that moment in great peril themselves. Selter, unaware of the secret provisions in the Nazi-Soviet Pact, courted the Germans. Before departing again for Moscow, he revealed to the German Minister in Estonia, Herr Frohwein, the substance of the Soviet demands and Estonia's proposed course of action. He asked that Ribbentrop be informed of the Estonian situation before the German Foreign

[1] German Foreign Office to German Embassy in USSR, September 27, 1939. *Documents, op. cit.,* p. 103.

Minister continued his conversations with Stalin and Molotov. Frohwein thereupon telegraphed the following information to the German Embassy in Moscow:[2]

"The Estonian Government, under the gravest threat of imminent attack, perforce is prepared to accept a military alliance with the Soviet Union. Selter will fly to Moscow tomorrow, Wednesday, to negotiate. Aim of negotiation: Framing of a treaty in such manner that the sovereignty and internal security of the country are preserved and the Estonian nonaggression pact kept intact. Hence they (the Estonians) intended to propose, in connection with the mutual assistance obligation of the contracting parties, to except the existing nonaggression pacts with third countries. It is further desired that naval and air bases should be made available only in case of war, when assistance obligation comes into play; in peace time as far as possible only preparation of the bases. The Russians first demanded Reval [Tallinn] as a naval base, but seem prepared to agree to Baltishport or the port of Osel. The Estonians wish if possible to grant air bases only on island. The general tendency is to meet the demands only as far as necessary to prevent an attack and maintain existing good relations with Germany."

Thus with high misgivings about the future of his country, Selter returned to Moscow on September 27. However his idea of negotiating an agreement evidently met with no approval in the Narkomindel; less than twenty-four hours later he signed a mutual assistance pact, and at Soviet terms.

Purportedly, the new pact was an extension of the Soviet-Estonian Peace Treaty of February 2, 1920. The two governments agreed to "render each other every assistance, including military assistance, in the event of direct aggression or a threat of aggression arising on the part of any great European power against the sea frontiers of the contracting parties on the Baltic Sea or against their land frontiers across the territory of the Latvian Republic." Estonia was not required to assist Russia directly in the event that the latter came into military conflict with any other power, but could hardly escape the consequences of such a conflict since the Russians were granted the right to maintain naval bases and military airfields on Estonian territory. The bases were leased to the USSR at "reasonable terms" and Soviet armed forces were to be of "strictly limited strength."

The most significant part of the agreement, however, was contained in Article 5: "The fulfillment of this pact must not affect in any measure

---

[2] Foreign Office to German Embassy in USSR, September 27, 1939, *Documents, op. cit.,* pp. 103-04.

the sovereign rights of the contracting parties, in particular their economic systems and state organizations." This article enabled the Estonians to save some aspect of honor. Doubtless few ever thought it necessary to insure Soviet sovereignty against Estonian encroachments, but on the other hand, this section of the agreement was hailed by pro-Soviet quarters as showing the good intentions of the USSR toward small nations. These same protagonists cited the articles as further proof that the Soviet Union had abandoned its revolutionary mission to Communize and Sovietize the world.

Almost immediately after the conclusion of the Estonian Pact, the Latvian Government was urgently requested by the Russians to send diplomatic representatives to Moscow. This request came as no surprise to the Latvians, who were apparently but unwillingly ready to accept any Soviet demands. Munters, the Latvian Minister of Foreign Affairs, arrived in Moscow on October 2, 1939. Three days later, on October 5, he signed an agreement which repeated almost word for word the text of the Soviet pact signed a week before with Estonia.

The economic, military, and political provisions were similar. Specifically, the Soviet Union was granted the right to establish naval bases at Libau and Windau, and airfields and artillery posts on the coast between Windau and Pitraga. As it had in Estonia, the Red Army began to occupy its new Latvian positions within three weeks after the conclusion of the pact.

Germany and the Soviet Union had not settled the question of partitioning Lithuania until the revised Secret Protocol of September 28, 1939. Even then it apparently was not settled to the full satisfaction of both parties. Complications arose early in October over both the return of Vilna to Lithuania, and the control of a small southwestern coastal sector within the German sphere of interest. On October 3, Molotov notified Schulenburg that the Soviet Government would inform the Lithuanian Foreign Minister, who was to arrive that day in Moscow, that the USSR was willing to cede the city of Vilna and its environs to Lithuania, and at the same time indicate to the Lithuanians that they in turn must cede the small southwestern coastal sector to Germany.

Schulenburg was naturally cool to Molotov's idea. "It seems to me," he told Molotov, "that the Soviet Government should exchange Vilna for the strip to be ceded to Germany and then hand this strip over to Germany."

Molotov of course was not in accord with this suggestion but agreed to wait until the following noon for an opinion from the German

Foreign Office. Schulenburg then wired Berlin the following analysis:[3]

"Molotov's suggestion seems to me harmful, as in the eyes of the world it would make us appear as robbers of Lithuanian territory, while the Soviet Government figures as the donor. As I see it, only my suggestion enters into consideration at all. However, I would ask you to consider whether it might not be advisable for us, by a separate secret German-Soviet protocol, to forego the cession of the Lithuanian strip of territory until the Soviet Union actually incorporates Lithuania, an idea on which, I believe, the arrangement concerning Lithuania was originally based."

By the following morning, Schulenburg had received a reply from Berlin, and immediately reported his latest instructions to Molotov. He asked that the Soviet Union not discuss this cession of territory with the Lithuanians for the time being, but rather assume the obligation toward Germany of leaving this strip of territory unoccupied by units of the Red Army until Germany determined the date on which the cession of the territory was to be formally effected. He requested that an understanding to this effect be set forth in a secret exchange of letters between himself and Molotov.

Molotov then replied that, unfortunately, he had been obliged the day before to inform the Lithuanian Foreign Minister of the original understanding, even though he had promised Schulenburg he would wait until the official German position had been expressed. "The Lithuanian delegation had been extremely dismayed and sad," said Molotov, and "had declared that the loss of this area in particular would be especially hard to bear, since many prominent leaders of the Lithuanian people came from that part of Lithuania." The Lithuanian Foreign Minister, continued Molotov, had that morning flown back to to Kowno with the preceding information.

Needless to say, this news was a source of great irritation to the German Foreign Office, which immediately sought to rectify the situation by a maneuver designed to nullify Molotov's supposedly accidental breach of faith. The German Minister in Kowno was instructed to notify the Lithuanian Foreign Minister that Germany had recommended to the USSR the cession of Vilna to Lithuania. In return for this arrangement, the German Government had reserved the right to a small strip of Lithuanian territory, but that it had not considered the question of border revision timely at the moment. The Lithuanian Foreign Minister appeared satisfied with this explanation. Molotov was then notified of the German action, and was asked to keep Soviet

[3] Schulenburg to Foreign Office, Oct. 3, 1939, *Documents, op. cit.*, p. 112.

"mutual assistance" troops clear of the area until Germany decided upon a date for the cession of the Lithuanian territory. The Kremlin quickly complied with this request in a secret exchange of letters on October 8, 1939.[4]

As finally adopted, the Soviet-Lithuanian treaty stated that "in order to strengthen the friendship between the USSR and Lithuania, the city of Vilno and the district of Vilno are hereby returned to the Republic of Lithuania by the USSR." The rest of the text was much the same as the previous pacts with Estonia and Latvia, except that the general character of the Lithuanian agreement gave a vague impression that the Soviet Union was dealing with an equally sovereign state. For instance, instead of direct military assistance in case of attack, the Lithuanian text provided for "mutual consultation" and the taking "of all measures as will be mutually agreed upon as necessary." The article which guaranteed the signatories' sovereign rights contained the pledge that Soviet Russia would pursue a policy of "noninterference in the internal affairs" of Lithuania. The military provisions were similar to those with Estonia and Latvia. Russia was granted the right to maintain land and air forces of a "strictly limited strength" on Lithuanian soil and in return granted equipment and supplies of a limited nature to the Lithuanian Army. But, as in the Estonian and Latvian Pacts, no definition of the words "strictly limited" was affixed to the agreement.

None the less, the pacts were favorably received by the Baltic peoples. They had anticipated possible extinction and were therefore pleasantly surprised when life continued much the same as it had before. There were, of course, certain good reasons why the Politburo permitted the independence of the Baltic states to continue at that time. First, if the Soviet Union had attempted forthright annexation and Sovietization, the move would doubtless have met with the suspicion and disapproval of the Germans. Even though the Baltic States were considered a part of the Soviet sphere, the tone of the Secret Protocol did not suggest immediate incorporation into the USSR. Second, the Politburo probably harbored some doubt as to whether Germany would be the eventual victor in the war. It will be recalled that both France and Great Britain maintained large and impressive armed forces until the early summer of 1940. Too aggressive a policy in the Baltic by the Soviet Government might have resulted in the loss of its neutrality. Soviet strategy, therefore, could best be served by

---

[4] For a complete account of these negotiations, see *Documents, op. cit.,* pp. 112-18.

tactics which permitted a maximum of flexibility to maneuver between the opposite possibilities of an Axis or an Allied victory.

In less than two months after the signing of the Nazi-Soviet Pact, the USSR had established a strong claim to the "Baltic Windows" which Peter the Great had once fought during two decades to win for Russia. Not a life was lost nor a shot fired. While Germany fought the war, the Soviet Union gathered in the spoils. Molotov sounded an ominous note when six months later he said "It must be admitted that the treaties between the Baltic States and the USSR have strengthened the position of all four of these nations. This creates premises for a further improvement in relations between the Soviet Union and the Baltic countries."[5]

From a defensive standpoint, still more land depth had been gained for the Red Army. The great strategic cities of Russia were that much farther from the starting point of an enemy attack. Moreover, through the acquisition of military bases, a strong position in the Baltic had been assured. The southern shores of the Gulf of Finland were in Russian hands—a consideration of great importance in the event of a conflict with the Finns. The ease with which the Baltic operation had transpired may have bred overconfidence. In any case, the remaining country in the Soviet sphere, Finland, was not to prove as amenable to Soviet designs.

[5] *Moscow News,* April 1, 1940.

CHAPTER 4

THE SOVIET-FINNISH WAR

"The Red Army is going to Finland to aid the Finnish people. Only the Soviet Union, which rejects in principle the forcible seizure of territory and the enslavement of peoples, could consent to lend its military might, not for aggression against Finland and for the enslavement of her people, but to secure Finnish independence, to increase the territory of Finland at the expense of the Soviet Union—to establish friendly relations with Finland."—"Pravda," December 4, 1939.

Even before the Soviet-Lithuanian Mutual Assistance Pact had gone into effect, Molotov indicated to the Finnish Minister in Moscow that the USSR was anxious to discuss a number of important questions concerning Finnish-Soviet relations. This was on October 5, 1939. From what the Finns had just witnessed in the Baltic States, there was of course little enthusiasm for any type of discussion with the Russians. Therefore the Finns were slow to reply and only after a second prompting by the Soviet minister in Helsinki did the Finnish envoy, Paasikivi, reluctantly depart for Moscow on October 11.

Negotiations the first day resulted in no written Russian demands. The Narkomindel merely suggested a pact of military assistance, an idea rejected categorically by the Finns who maintained that it would lead eventually to Soviet occupation of their country. At the next conference, however, the Soviets were more definitive. They presented the Finns with a written demand for boundary adjustments and territorial concessions. These demands consisted of the following:

1. The Port of Hanko to be leased to Russia with the right to maintain a Red Army garrison of up to 5,000 men.

2. The Port of Lappohja to be made available to the USSR for use as a Soviet naval anchorage.

3. Five islands in the Gulf of Finland and 2,761 square kilometers in the Karelian Isthmus to be ceded to the USSR.

4. The USSR to cede to Finland, in return, 5,529 square kilometers in Central Karelia.

5. The northern frontier to be adjusted in the region of the Arctic Ocean.

6. The Finnish-Soviet border to be demilitarized and all fortifications demolished.

7. Neither party to enter into any international alliance aimed at the other contracting party.

Soon after he had received these proposals, Paasikivi, the Finnish envoy returned to Helsinki. Ten days later, after continuous cabinet consultations, the Finns presented counter-proposals to the USSR. These represented a compromise with the Russian demands. The Finns agreed to cede four islands in the Gulf of Finland, to move the frontier in the vicinity of Leningrad 13 kilometers away from the existing border (but not to destroy existing Mannerheim fortifications), to reaffirm the nonaggression treaty then in force, and to reject proposals for the lease or cession of Hanko. The proposals were unacceptable to the Russians and although a few more concessions were made at subsequent parleys, the negotiations then came practically to a standstill. The stumbling blocks to a joint agreement appear to have been the question of Hanko, which the Russians repeatedly demanded and which the Finns flatly refused to relinquish, and the question of the Mannerheim fortifications on the isthmus fronting Leningrad.

As Frederick L. Schuman put it, "The stakes of diplomacy judged worth fighting for, here as always, were the factors decisively affecting future fighting capacity."[1] The Finns could not consent to yield those elements of power whose surrender would seriously impair their ability to resist future Soviet demands. Nor could the Russians although they did not advance the idea at the time, afford to leave strategic Leningrad vulnerable to possible attack by Anglo-French or German forces.

Negotiations were finally broken off on November 13, at least partially as a result of a threatening speech made a few days earlier by Foreign Minister Molotov. The Soviet press then began to bombard the obstinate Finns with such slogans as "The patience of the Soviet people will come to an end!!" and "We are ready to give a stern lesson!"[2] Nevertheless, the Finns remained adamant.

Having failed to secure its aims by negotiation, the Politburo resorted to a border incident. On November 26, 1939, the Finnish Government was informed by a Russian note that on that very day Soviet troops, stationed on the Isthmus of Karelia near the village of Mainila,

[1] Frederick L. Schuman, *Soviet Politics at Home and Abroad*, (New York, 1948), p. 386.

[2] *Ibid.*, p. 387.

"were suddenly subjected to artillery fire from Finnish territory." The Soviet Government, said the note, feels "that concentration of Finnish troops near Leningrad not only creates a menace for Leningrad, but in actual fact represents a hostile act against the USSR and has already led to an attack on Soviet troops and to loss of life." The Russians then demanded that the Finnish Government withdraw its troops 25 kilometers away from the Karelian Isthmus frontier.

The Finns rejected the Soviet note, but proposed that a mixed commission be instructed to carry out an inquiry into the incident. Molotov refused to accept this proposal. Instead he presented a note to the Finnish Minister in Moscow informing him that the Soviet Government no longer recognized the USSR-Finnish Treaty of Nonaggression. Two days later, November 30, 1939, Soviet planes bombed Helsinki and Red Army troops crossed the Finnish frontier. But the quick victory planned in the Kremlin did not materialize. The stubborn Finns offered continued and admirable resistance against overwhelming odds.

At this same time, the Soviet leaders resorted to a technique used almost two decades earlier in Poland: the establishment of a puppet government in Russia in order to legitimatize and advance Soviet designs for aggrandizement. In this case, it was the revolutionary Finnish "People's Government"—supposedly operating in the Finnish border town of Terijoki, but in fact operating in Moscow. This government was headed by Otto Kuusinen, a Finnish Communist who had last seen Finland some twenty years earlier as he was fleeing toward Russia to escape the wrath of Finnish counter-revolutionary forces.

On December 1, Tass, the Soviet news agency, announced that "the chairman of the Finnish People's Government and Minister for Foreign Affairs, M. Kuusinen, officially informed the Praesidium of the Supreme Soviet of the USSR of the formation of the "People's Government of Finland" and requested the establishment of diplomatic relations between the Democratic Republic of Finland and the Soviet Union. "The Praesidium," the Tass report continued, "has decided to recognize the People's Government of Finland and to establish diplomatic relations between the USSR and the Democratic Republic of Finland."[3]

Immediately after it had been so recognized the Kuusinen government declared: "The People's Government of Finland, being deeply convinced that the Soviet Union pursues no aims contrary to the independence of our country, fully approves and supports actions by the Red Army on the territory of Finland. It regards them as invaluable

[3] *Pravda,* December 1, 1939; *New York Times,* December 2, 1939.

assistance to the Finnish people on the part of the Soviet Union . . . the People's Government invites the Government of the USSR to render the Democratic Republic of Finland all necessary assistance by the Red Army forces." [4]

On the third day of its existence, the People's Government of Finland signed an agreement with the USSR which in many ways was similar to the pacts negotiated by the Soviet Union with the Baltic States, except, of course, for its territorial provisions. By terms of the agreement, the People's Government not only consented to an adjustment of the frontier on the Karelian Isthmus north of Leningrad favorable to Russia, but also ceded other Finnish territory amounting to 3,970 kilometers. In exchange, the USSR consented to transfer to the Kuusinen regime some 70,000 square kilometers of territory in Soviet Karelia containing a predominantly Karelian population. This was more than twelve times the 5,529 square kilometers that the Narkomindel had previously offered in negotiations with the legitimate Finnish Government. As it worked out, this area, supposedly ceded by the USSR, was almost the only territory controlled by the People's Government during the Soviet-Finnish war. The Kremlin's purpose, naturally, was to give a slight hue of legitimacy to its Finnish puppet regime.

Other areas transferred to Russian sovereignty by the Communist Finns included five islands in the Gulf of Finland, parts of the Rybachi and Srendi peninsulas on the Arctic coast, a railway line on the Karelian Isthmus (sold to the Russians for 120,000,000 Finnish marks) and the Hanko Peninsula and its surrounding territorial waters. The USSR agreed to pay 300,000,000 Finnish marks to the Kuusinen People's Government for its new territorial acquisitions.

Meanwhile, the legal Finnish government in Helsinki had begun— and was to continue—to search for ways of negotiating peace. The Finns were aided (or hindered) in their efforts not only by most of the great powers in Europe and the Scandinavian countries, but by the United States as well. For Russia, on the other hand, the entire plan for the Finnish operation, and there is some question if there was a military plan, went counterwise to expectations. Instead of a quick military conquest, the battle dragged on and on. Moreover, the Red Army incurred tremendous casualties and an equally tremendous loss of prestige. The men in the Politburo—alone responsible for the entire fiasco—cantankerously refused to negotiate with the "Mannerheim White Guard Gangsters," as they called the Helsinki Government, but

4 *Pravda,* December 1, 1939; *New York Times,* December 2, 1939.

instead carried on discussions with their own echo—the Kuusinen group.

There was no question at all that in time the Red Army by sheer size alone—no matter how capable and heroic its opponents—would overrun Finland. However, the USSR did not choose to wait for such a triumph. Instead, from the middle of January 1940, every effort was made to conclude the war as quickly as possible, so long as at least a slight victory could be claimed. The reason was that this purely local engagement gave every indication of exploding into a large-scale war. Britain and France were in the process of completing arrangements to come to the aid of the Finns from early in 1941 on. The Soviet Union at that time had no desire for war with the Anglo-French combine, and doubtless as little desire to be allied with Germany in the event of such a struggle. Moscow craved neutrality, and the fruits of neutrality. The German Ambassador in Moscow, Schulenburg, noted in a telegram to his Foreign Office in late March after hostilities had ended that "the Soviet Government is determined to cling to neutrality in the present war and to avoid as much as possible anything that might involve it in a conflict with the Western Powers. This must have been one of the main reasons why the Soviet Government broke off the war against Finland. . . ."[5]

The break in the war came amidst rumors of all types of intrigue involving Britain, France, the Scandinavian countries, and Germany. Early in March 1940, shortly after the USSR had abandoned the myth of negotiating solely with the Kuusinen People's Government, a Finnish peace delegation departed secretly for Moscow. Its mission was successful. On March 12 a peace treaty was signed, and hostilities ceased the following day at noon.

The tragedy of the treaty was that after 104 days of fighting and the loss of thousands of lives, the terms were practically the same as those insisted upon by Soviet Russia during the previous October and November. Finland was forced to cede all of the Karelian Isthmus (including the city of Viborg and Viborg Bay with its islands), territories to the north and west of Lake Ladoga (including the cities of Sortavala and Keksholm), to grant border adjustments in favor of Russia in the Kandalaksha region, and to surrender the Rybachi and Srendni peninsulas as well as several islands in the Gulf of Finland. Moreover, the Soviets gained free transit to and from Norway through the Petsamo area and a thirty-year lease with the right to maintain

[5] Schulenburg to German Foreign Office, March 30, 1940, *Documents, op. cit.*, pp. 135-6.

naval, land and air forces on the Hanko Peninsula and the nearby islands for an annual rental of eight million Finnish marks (approximately $330,000). The Helsinki Government was compelled to reaffirm the Soviet-Finnish Treaty of 1920, which limited its warships and armed vessels in the Arctic area, and at the same time to agree that no submarines and military aircraft would be allowed in waters of the Petsamo region. As doubtful compensation, the USSR restored to Finland part of the seized Petsamo area including its port facilities and its nickel mines.

Thus in the final analysis, even though the Soviet Government had ended the war hurriedly, it had still realized its original territorial ambitions. According to Molotov, "The conclusion of the Peace Treaty with Finland consummates the task we set ourselves last year of safeguarding the security of the Soviet Union in the direction of the Baltic."[6]

Apparently, however, Molotov was not unmindful of the fact that the threat of British and French intervention had cost the USSR the whole of Finland and had forced her to scrap the government of Kuusinen. Somewhat bitterly, he referred to certain elements in the governments of the western nations who had not approved of the Russian attempt at expansion. Before the Sixth Session of the Supreme Soviet, he said: "To this should be added that amidst this furious howling of the enemies of the Soviet Union, always loudest of all were the squealing voices of all those prostituted Socialists of the Second International [lively animation in the hall], all those Attlees and Blums, Citrines and Jouhaux, Tranmaels and Hoglunds—all those lackeys of capital who have sold themselves body and soul to the warmongers." Not content with that, Molotov went on and perhaps inadvertently revealed an important, often forgotten concept of Soviet foreign policy. "It is time that these gentry understood," he said, "that the USSR has always pursued its own policy and always will pursue it, irrespective of whether these gentry in other countries like it or not." (Stormy prolonged applause.)[7]

The Kuusinen Government, upon which Moscow had based so many plans, was pushed far to the background when the Politburo decided that the war had to end quickly. Its major wartime operations had consisted of publishing an anti-Helsinki newspaper, issuing volumes

[6] Molotov, before the Sixth Session of the Supreme Soviet, *Moscow News*, April 1, 1940.

[7] Ibid. Molotov's remarks were reminiscent of Bismarck's, "Wir Deutschen furehten Gott, und nichts alter in der Welt"—"We Germans fear God and no one else in the World."

of printed matter denouncing the "Mannerheim clique", and making periodic radio broadcasts glorifying the Soviet Union and damning Finnish warmongers. One of its principal projects had been the organization of the "First Army Corps of the Democratic Republic of Finland" which, according to the People's Government, was designed to "receive reinforcements by volunteers from among the revolutionary workers and farmers, and become the strong backbone of the future People's Army of Finland." This Army Corps was to "be accorded the honor of carrying the banner of Finland's Democratic Republic into the capital and of raising it over the Presidential Palace to the joy of the toiling people and to the awe of the enemies of the people."[8] There is considerable doubt, however, that the "First Army Corps" lived up to expectations. The first reports of the group in action came on February 25, a few days before the war ended.

Another project of the Kuusinen regime consisted of organizing workers committees in the few towns which, after capture by the Red Army, came into People's Government hands. It was unnecessary, of course, to do any organizing in the areas ceded to the puppet republic by the USSR; these territories had been for some time well organized by the Russian Soviet Republic. Whether any organic change occurred because of the ostensible change in sovereignty is hard to determine.

The Kuusinen People's Democracy somehow tired of war and bloodshed at the same time as did the USSR. As Molotov declared before the Supreme Soviet on March 18, 1940, at the ratification of the Peace Treaty with Finland: "The Finnish People's Government in order to avert bloodshed and to alleviate the burdens of the Finnish people, agreed that every effort should be made to bring the war to an end at once. The question of dissolving the People's Government then arose. This it has already done of its own volition."

Although the People's Government was dissolved, the "Democratic Republic of Finland" was not. On the contrary, two weeks after the end of the war, on March 31, 1940, the Supreme Soviet of the USSR united the Karelian Autonomous Republic (a unit of the Russian Soviet Republic) with those areas which had been ceded by Finland, and thus constructed a Union Republic—the Soviet Karelo-Finnish Socialist Republic. This in fact was an actual continuation of the Democratic Republic of Finland.

The Supreme Soviet was making good use of its nationality policy and the federal union aspect of the USSR constitution. A new Finnish state had been created by Moscow which would have obvious advan-

8 *Pravda,* December 1, 1939; *New York Times,* December 2, 1939.

tages in future dealings with the Finns of the "White Guard Manner-heim Gang." Indicative of continuing Soviet interest in the future of Finland, Otto Kuusinen, leader of the puppet regime, retained his former position as president by becoming Chairman of the Praesidium of the Supreme Soviet of the Karelo-Finnish Republic during the following July.

While Soviet strategy in Finland was ostensibly based on the desire for security, the Kremlin also sought to take advantage of the benefits accruing to it from the Secret Protocol of the Nonaggression Treaty. Overconfidence seems to have developed in the Politburo from the ease with which the Soviet Union scored repeated successes in Poland, Estonia, Latvia, and Lithuania. Obviously Russia had not counted on two things: Finnish resistance to her demands, and a drawn out war with the resulting complications. The manner in which the entire affair had been handled was a characteristic of Soviet diplomacy, and a permanent reminder of the disregard for treaty obligations that the Soviet Government is capable of exercising.

Communist spokesmen have justified the means by the end-objective of defense against the eventual German attack. In this regard, the Soviet radio on June 26, 1941 stated that the cause of the Finnish war was the presence of an aggressor who "had compelled the Soviet Union to seek security by reverting to the old policy of securing strategic positions. It was obviously not against Finland that the USSR needed to take precautions," the Soviet speaker admitted, "but it was realized that Germany could have used Finnish territory for an attack on the Soviet Union."[9] Such a *modus operandi*, however, has dangerous complications if carried to any extreme in international relations.

Strategically, of course, the Finnish war resulted in great gains for Soviet Russia. The approaches to vital Leningrad from land and sea were secured. Defense in the northwest was henceforth guaranteed by the lakes and elevated ground of the Karelo-Finnish Union Republic. Finland appeared to have been eliminated as an area from which a hostile attack could be launched against the USSR.

In both the theoretical and factual expansion of Communism, how-ever, the Politburo had not succeeded. The small areas wrested from Finland were little compensation for the hatred of the Finns, and the suspicions generated in other nations. It was doubtful if anything but the force of the Red Army would ever bring about Russianism or Communism in Finland.

There were two primary techniques that characterized Soviet action

[9] *Times*, London, June 27, 1941.

in Finland. The first of these was the creation of the puppet govern-ment headed by Otto Kuusinen, and the second was the manipulation of the multi-national federal structure of the Soviet Union used to combine Soviet Finland with Soviet Karelia. Both were employed against Finland to establish legitimacy of action in much the same way, for instance, as were Soviet plebiscites and elections in partitioned Poland. In this case, the Politburo doubtless intended to use the Peo-ple's Republic to carry through any and all measures of the Supreme Soviet once the Red Army had overrun Finland. Such projected actions, however, were to be represented as the free will of the people of Fin-land acting in harmony with the free peoples of the Soviet Union. Dictates would apparently not be construed as Kremlin inspired, but rather as the collective decisions of the people of a sovereign state. The evolution of the Finnish Democratic Republic and the Karelo Autonomous Republic into the Karelo-Finnish Soviet Republic estab-lished a basis for an eventual expansion to include all Finns, under the guise of liberating "the kindred Finn brothers from White Guard enslavement." Theoretically, the system appeared flawless. It could and would be used again and again.

CHAPTER 5

THE BALTIC COUP DE GRACE

"The rush for the spoils had begun. But Mussolini was not the only hungry animal seeking prey. To join the jackal came the bear."—Winston Churchill, "Their Finest Hour."

The era of brotherly feeling between Germany and the Soviet Union that had been born with the signing of the Nonaggression Pact in August 1939 began to deteriorate early in 1940. Moscow, not Berlin, decided that the alliance might lead to unmanageable complications. When the conflict with Finland continued beyond the few days originally anticipated, the Russians observed anxiously that the unfriendly attitude of the Anglo-French alliance increased daily. During the latter part of February and early March 1940, this antagonism increased until the Allied Powers were ready to dispatch an expeditionary force to aid the Finns, and possibly to declare war on the USSR. This possibility in turn strongly influenced the Kremlin to quickly end the Finnish War even though the Red Army had at long last begun to win long overdue battles.[1] Indirectly, therefore, the Allies doubtless saved the Finns from a peace like that of Brest-Litovsk.

The Politburo fully realized, moreover, that a continuation of the war with Finland could easily be catastrophic to the Soviet policy of lucrative neutrality in World War II. The thought of being an active ally of Nazi Germany could have been even more upsetting to the Russians, especially since Britain and France then appeared as powerful antagonists. In actual fact, considerably before the Finnish War was brought to a close, the USSR began to pursue strict neutrality even toward its ally Germany.

The Politburo would not soon forget that the Finnish phase of its opportunistic foreign policy had nearly been disastrous. From that moment on, every precaution was taken to see that a similar situation did not again arise.

[1] See Chapter 4, footnote number 5. *Documents, op. cit.,* pp. 135-6.

The apparent cooling of the Nazi-Soviet friendship changed, however, to one of renewed good fellowship when the German Army overran Denmark and Norway. Schulenburg, Germany's Ambassador to the USSR, commented penetratingly on this subject in a memorandum dated April 11, 1939:

"For some time we have observed in the Soviet Government a distinct shift which was unfavorable to us. In all fields we suddenly came up against obstacles which were, in many cases, completely unnecessary. . . . These obstacles, which were apparent everywhere, reached their climax in the suspension of petroleum and grain shipments. . . . We asked ourselves in vain what the reason might be for the sudden change of attitude of the Soviet authorities. After all, nothing at all had happened! I suspect that the tremendous clamour of our enemies and their sharp attacks on neutrals—particularly on the Soviet Union —and on neutrality in general were not without effect upon the Soviet Government, so that it feared being forced by the Entente into a great war for which it is not prepared, and that for this reason it wanted to avoid anything that might have furnished a pretext to the English and French for reproaching the Soviet Union with unneutral behavior or partisanship for Germany . . . the situation had become so critical that I decided to call on Molotov in order to talk these matters over with him, and after this discussion to notify the Foreign Office. On the 8th of this month I therefore asked for permission to see Molotov—i.e., *before* the Scandinavian events. Actually the visit to Molotov did not take place until the morning of the 9th—i.e., *after* our Scandinavian operations. During this talk it became apparent that the Soviet Government had again made a complete about-face. Suddenly the suspension of the petroleum and grain shipments was termed 'excessive zeal of subordinate agencies' which would be immediately remedied.

"In my opinion there is only one explanation for this about-face: our Scandinavian operations must have relieved the Soviet Government enormously—removed a great burden of anxiety, so to speak. What their apprehension consisted of, can again not be determined with certainty. I suspect the following: The Soviet Government is always extraordinarily well informed. If the English and French intended to occupy Norway and Sweden it may be assumed with certainty that the Soviet Government knew of these plans and was apparently terrified by them. The Soviet Government saw the English and French appearing on the shores of the Baltic Sea, and they saw the Finnish question reopened, as Lord Halifax announced; finally they dreaded most of all the danger of becoming involved in a war with two Great Powers.

Apparently this fear was relieved by us. Only in this way can the completely changed attitude of Herr Molotov be understood."[2]

Thus for a short while the Soviet Union and Germany again enjoyed the friendliest of relations. In fact, with each succeeding operation of the German Army, the Politburo was apparently more pleased. Molotov, when informed of the Nazis' Scandinavian operation, told Schulenburg, "We wish Germany complete success in her defensive measures."[3] Later, when informed of Hitler's attack against the Low Countries, Molotov added that he understood Germany had to protect herself against an Anglo-French attack, and that he had no doubt of German success.[4]

During the spring and early summer of 1940 Germany was almost wholly occupied in the west, thus providing an opportune moment for Soviet Russia to act further in her designated sphere of influence. Losing little time the USSR informed Lithuania on May 28, 1940, that a number of Red Army soldiers had mysteriously disappeared from a Russian tank brigade in that country. One of these soldiers, said the Soviets, had been kidnapped and threatened with death if he refused to tell Lithuanian authorities the strength of his brigade. Another soldier, continued the Soviets, had obviously been murdered and was not, as the Lithuanian authorities maintained, a suicide.

The Russian note, however, was not accompanied by any specific demands. As a safeguard, the Lithuanians suggested that a mixed commission investigate the incidents, but, needless to say, the idea was rejected by the Soviet Government. The Lithuanians then took several measures designed to satisfy the Moscow authorities. All citizens were immediately evacuated from areas in which Russian tank brigades were stationed and a special commission was appointed to investigate the alleged crimes. These measures, however, did not satisfy the USSR. Lithuania then hopefully suggested that she send her Foreign Minister to Moscow for discussions, but Russia insisted instead that the Lithuanian Prime Minister himself be sent to negotiate.

Merkys, the Lithuanian Prime Minister, therefore departed for Moscow and held his first conversation with Molotov on June 7, 1940. He was reproached severely by the Russian for not taking adequate measures to guarantee the safety of Soviet troops, but at that time he was not informed of the real reason for his presence in Moscow. Not until June 9 did Molotov get to the point of Merkys' visit. A military

[2] Memorandum by Schulenburg, April 11, 1940, *Documents, op. cit.,* pp. 138-40.

[3] *Ibid.,* Schulenburg to Foreign Office, April 9, 1940, p. 138.

[4] *Ibid.,* May 10, 1940, *op. cit.,* p. 142.

alliance, Molotov insinuated, existed between the three Baltic states, and as proof of this supposition, he pointed out that frequent meetings had been held between military and diplomatic heads of the three countries.

Merkys replied that there were neither secret nor open agreements which violated the letter or spirit of the 1939 Soviet-Lithuanian Mutual Assistance Pact; Molotov seemed completely satisfied with this reply. Merkys therefore returned to Kaunas, on June 12, 1940, with Russian assurance that relations between the two countries would continue to be governed by the existing mutual assistance agreement. Apparently the Narkomindel had not yet decided on a final course of action in the Baltic.

Almost immediately after the Merkys-Molotov conversations, however, the military situation in France changed drastically. Perhaps as a result of the change, only two days after his return from Moscow, Merkys was handed a new note by the Soviet Minister in Lithuania. This note repeated the gist of what had just been discussed in Moscow, but added that terrorist acts against Red Army men had been committed with the intention of making it impossible for Soviet military forces to remain in Lithuania, and had been undertaken primarily "to foster hostility toward Soviet military employees, and to instigate excesses against Red Army forces." These facts, continued the note, "indicate clearly that the Lithuanian Government is violating its mutual assistance agreement with Soviet Russia and is preparing an attack upon the Soviet garrisons situated in Lithuania."[5]

In addition, the Lithuanian Government was once again accused of entering into a military alliance with Latvia and Estonia directed against the Soviet Union. Soviet Russia therefore demanded that certain measures be carried out immediately. These measures included the immediate trial of the Minister of Internal Affairs and Chief of the Political Police, the formation of a new government able to carry out the Mutual Assistance Pact, and Lithuanian consent to the stationing of Red Army troops in important centers of the country. The Red Army contingents were to be large enough to assure fulfillment of agreements entered into by the two countries. Lithuania was given until ten the following morning to make a satisfactory reply.

Shortly before the deadline, Lithuania, with little opportunity to do otherwise, capitulated to the Soviet demands. The government in power then resigned, while additional units of the Red Army rolled across the Lithuanian frontier. According to reports, the next few days

[5] *Moscow News,* June 19, 1940.

were ones of complete confusion, with literally no government in operation.

Aware that their existence hung in the balance, several prominent Lithuanian officials fled to Germany. The night duty officer of the German Foreign Office reported early on June 16, 1940, that he had received a call from the Lithuanian Minister about 2 A.M., reporting that the Lithuanian President, Smetona, his family and entourage had arrived at the Lithuanian-German frontier and desired to enter Germany. In addition, the Lithuanian Minister had revealed, a number of other prominent Lithuanians were seeking to cross the frontier, fearing severe castigation if they fell into the hands of the Russians. The Lithuanian Minister had then requested that German border authorities be instructed to allow these people to pass into Germany along with various detachments and regiments of the Lithuanian Army. His request was immediately granted by Ribbentrop who gave orders to allow, but not to encourage, Lithuanian Army personnel and civilians to enter Germany.[6] Meanwhile, amidst this confusion, the Soviet Government dispatched its Assistant Commissar for Foreign Affairs, Dekanozov, to organize a friendly regime in Lithuania. Experienced observers felt that it would be but a short time until that country was a part of the Soviet Union.

In the two Baltic states to the north, events similar to those in Lithuania were transpiring. Two days after the Soviet ultimatum to Lithuania, Molotov delivered similar demands to the Estonian and Latvian Ministers in Moscow. The notes were couched in identical language and accused the two Baltic Republics of an alliance dangerous to the frontiers of the USSR. Molotov demanded that Estonia and Latvia immediately form new regimes capable of carrying out the terms of the 1939 Mutual Assistance Pacts, and that both governments allow Red Army troops free movement within their territories. There was no alternative but for the two nations to comply at once. The governments in power resigned and a short period of chaos resulted similar to that which had existed earlier in Lithuania. At this moment, the USSR, as always professing interest in the peaceful well-being of its neighboring nations, dispatched Zhdanov to Estonia and Vishinsky to Latvia to assist in the reorganization of the two nations.

In justifying this Soviet interference, on August 1, Molotov expressed his regrets that the conclusion of nonaggression pacts in 1939 had not produced the desired results and had not led to "the rapprochement between these states and the Soviet Union that might have been

6 *Documents, op. cit.,* pp. 148-49.

expected. Ruling groups," he said, "took the road of intensifying hostile activities pursued secretly and behind the back of the USSR. For this purpose was utilized the so-called Baltic Entente, which at the end of last year [1939] was converted into a military alliance including Lithuania as well as Latvia and Estonia. . . . This proves," continued Molotov, "that the ruling bourgeois groups were incapable of honestly carrying out the acts of mutual assistance concluded with the Soviet, that, on the contrary, they even extended their hostile activities against the Soviet. Facts proving that these countries were crudely violating the pacts kept piling up. It became utterly impossible to tolerate such a state of affairs any longer, particularly in the present international situation. This was the reason why the Soviet Government presented the demands that you know concerning changes in the governments of these states and the dispatch of additional Red Army units to these countries. The results of these steps are known to you."[7]

These "results" provided an unequivocal object lesson to other states bordering on or having close relations with the Soviet Union. On the questionable pretense that the USSR expected an attack from these small bourgeois-controlled governments, Moscow thrice violated its pledge of non-interference and brusquely installed puppet regimes.

The governments picked initially by Dekanozov, Zhdanov, and Vishinsky were not entirely Communist, but were, however, composed of extreme left-wing political elements. As was to be expected, these new regimes described their first aim as collaboration and friendship with the Soviet Union. In concert, they announced dissolution of the existing parliaments, new elections, amnesties for left-wing political prisoners, democratic rights for all citizens, and plans for the improvement of the social and economic systems. At the same time a one-party press was installed and the armies of the Baltic states were reorganized into "People's Armies." Moreover, in accordance with Soviet wishes, the puppet governments of Latvia and Estonia also renounced both the military assistance pact of 1923 and their alliance of 1934. These two agreements, it will be recalled, had been the Soviet pretext for interference and overthrow of the legitimate governments of the Baltic republics.

To give an air of legality to Soviet acts, new elections in the three countries were set for July 14 and 15, 1940. Only Communist-approved delegates from Soviet-organized social organizations were allowed to be candidates. They in turn ran under the party heading "Union of the

[7] *Moscow News*, August 2, 1940.

Toiling People", a self-explanatory title. The chief demands put forward by this group were for inviolability of the USSR (not their own countries) and for far-reaching economic and social legislation. Election propaganda consisted mainly of praise for the great leader Stalin and the heroic Red Army. It was subsequently a surprise to no one that when the elections were over and the ballots counted, all three nations had given better than ninety percent of their respective votes to the "Union of the Toiling People."

It was an equally small surprise when, on July 21, less than a week after the elections, the parliaments of the three nations met in special sessions and, under the apparent insistence of the toiling people, voted to introduce the Soviet system into their countries and to apply for admission to the USSR. The resolutions of the three nations, presumably adopted independently of each other, stated that they desired to be admitted into the Soviet Union as fraternal republics "on the same basis that the Ukrainian, White Russian, and other fraternal republics were admitted to the Union."

Only two weeks later the request of the new Baltic Communist regimes was granted at the Seventh Session of the Supreme Soviet in Moscow. At this gathering, Molotov attempted to establish a modicum of legitimacy for these seizures:

"The most important measure carried out by these governments friendly to the Soviet that were set up in Estonia, Latvia, and Lithuania, was the holding of free parliamentary elections. The Seims of Lithuania and Latvia, and the State Assembly of Estonia, elected on the basis of universal, direct and equal suffrage, with secret ballot, have already expressed their unanimous opinion on fundamental political questions. We can note with satisfaction that the peoples of these countries voted solidly for their representatives, who have unanimously expressed themselves in favor of the introduction of the Soviet system and the incorporation of their nations into the Union of Soviet Socialist Republics." (Stormy applause.)

(These nations) "will greatly enhance their strength, increase their security and, at the same time, increase still further the might of the Great Soviet Union." (Stormy prolonged applause.)

"The fact that the frontier will now be moved to the Baltic Coast is of paramount importance to our country. At the same time, we shall now have ice-free ports in the Baltic, of which we stand in such great need.

"The successes of the foreign policy of the Soviet Union are all the more significant in that we have achieved them all by peaceful settlement. . . ."[8]

Lithuania was incorporated to the Soviet Union August 1, Latvia on August 5, and Estonia on August 8, 1940, as the fourteenth, fifteenth, and sixteenth Soviet Union Republics. Immediately, these three new Soviets nationalized all land, banks, and factories, although small holdings were temporarily left in the hands of private owners and collectivization was not initially attempted. The Soviet economic and social program gave initial indications of following that of the New Economic Policy used in the USSR during the nineteen-twenties.

Thus, the final moves of the Soviet Union in the Baltic area were quick and deadly. The Politburo waited patiently until Germany was occupied in the west with France and Britain and then carried out the Baltic *coup de grace*. Once again the ostensible basis for Soviet action was security. In addition, however, the Kremlin was anxious to legalize territorial seizures within its sphere of influence. The Baltic region, which a quarter of a century earlier had been Tsarist Russia's, was triumphantly restored to Soviet Russia. A "window" on the Baltic had been opened. The USSR achieved, as Molotov said, "ice free ports of which we have such great need." Furthermore, Communist doctrine expanded with territorial acquisition. The 66,800 square miles of territory and 5,998,000 people that were affixed to the USSR were simultaneously liberated from "capitalist enslavement" and returned to the control of the "toiling masses."

The methods employed were perhaps crude, but Soviet historians were provided with the necessary basis of legitimacy all the way through, and including a "spontaneous" desire of the aggrandized states to become Soviet Republics. Soviet history would not record, however, that the presence of the Red Army made it impossible for the Baltic states to resist, or negotiate on an equal basis, that the Soviet notes had been in the form of ultimatums, that the presence of Zhdanov, Dekanozov, and Vishinsky constituted direct interference in the internal affairs of the Baltic republics.

All in all, the Red Army was doubtless the indispensable instrument of aggrandizement: its presence facilitated subsequent actions which otherwise could not have proceeded with such ease. Subsequently, Soviet constitutional provisions for the admittance of new states made possible the quick absorption of new Soviet regimes and added that measure of legitimacy always sought for in Kremlin actions of this type.

8 *Moscow News,* August 2, 1940.

The time in which these startling acts of aggrandizement were accomplished was less than two weeks. When the world looked briefly away from the tragedy of June 1940, the Soviet Union presented it with a *fait accompli* in the Baltic. But it was not the only swift Soviet seizure of this period. With equal quickness the Politburo soon struck in the Balkans.

CHAPTER 6

NAZI-SOVIET PACT: BESSARABIA AND NORTHERN BUCOVINA

"Permit me now to turn to those problems of our foreign policy the successful solution of which has recently brought about a considerable expansion of our territory and augmented the forces of the Soviet Union."—Molotov, August 2, 1940.

The Politburo obviously believed that if the Soviet Union were to realize its long-standing claim to Bessarabia it would have to do so before the close of the historic month of June, 1940. Germany was consolidating her position in the west and would soon be turning increased attention to the east. In fact, German influence in Rumania was strong by the middle of June and showed evidence of becoming increasingly predominant.

In view of the circumstances, the Kremlin felt compelled to act. On the night of June 23 Molotov summoned the German Ambassador, Schulenburg, and informed him that "the solution of the Bessarabian question brooked no further delay." He stated that although the USSR was striving for a peaceful solution, it was determined to use force should the Rumanians decline Kremlin terms for a peaceful settlement. Furthermore, he told the amazed German Ambassador, the Soviet claim would extend to Bucovina as well as Bessarabia. As justification for this sudden Russian action, Molotov declared merely that a long time had elapsed since his declaration before the Supreme Soviet on April 1, 1940,[1] and Rumania had done nothing to bring about a solution to the problem. Therefore, something would have to be done.

[1] Molotov's declaration on April 1, 1940 was as follows: ". . . Of the . . . southern neighboring states, Rumania is the one with which we have no pact of nonaggression. This is due to the existence of a dispute that has not been settled, the question of Bessarabia, whose seizure by Rumania the Soviet Union has never recognized, although it never raised the question of recovering Bessarabia by military means. Hence there are no grounds for any deterioration in Soviet-Rumanian relations." *Moscow News*, April 1, 1940. Historically, Russia had seized Bessarabia in 1812 from

Schulenburg expressed complete surprise. He was aware, he said, that the USSR would maintain its claims to Bessarabia, but did not realize that the Soviets intended to take the initiative toward immediate realization of these claims. He asked Molotov to withhold action until he had informed the German Foreign Office. Molotov replied only that he would inform the Politburo of the request, but that the matter was extremely urgent and that Soviet action was imminent.

After hurried consultations between Hitler and Ribbentrop, instructions were given Schulenburg on June 25 to inform Molotov that Germany would abide by the August 1939 Secret Protocol and would take no interest in the Bessarabian question. The Germans informed the Soviet Union that they did, however, reserve the right to make certain proposals concerning the fate of the *Volksdeutsche* in the area. But the Soviet claim for Bucovina, Germany protested, was something new. It was pointed out to the Kremlin that this territory was formerly an Austrian crown province and was densely populated with Germans. The German Government, therefore, did not look with favor on the Soviet claim. Schulenburg informed Molotov that if the Soviet Government should renounce its claim to Bucovina, which had never belonged even to Tsarist Russia, "it would substantially facilitate a peaceful solution." Molotov countered by saying that Bucovina was the last missing part of a unified Ukraine and that for this reason the Soviet had decided to limit its demand to the northern part of Bucovina and the city of Chernovtsy. He suggested that the boundary line run from the southernmost point of the Soviet West Ukraine at Mt. Kniatiasa, east along the Suczava and then northeast to Hertza on the Pruth, where the Soviet Union would obtain a direct railway connection from Bessarabia via Chernovtsy to Lwow. Germany, under the pressure of events in Western Europe, was compelled to agree to this adjustment.[2]

As soon as Schulenburg had given the reluctant German approval, Molotov summoned the Rumanian Minister in Moscow and presented him with a lengthy note. The essence of this communiqué stated that

---

Turkey, and controlled the greater part of it until the collapse of the Imperial Government in 1917. In February 1918, the area declared itself the Moldavian Republic. The following March, Bucharest and Moscow concluded an agreement whereby Rumanian troops then occupying the area would be withdrawn within two months. Three weeks later the governing council of Moldavia, perhaps influenced by the presence of Rumanian troops, voted to unite with the Kingdom of Rumania. At the time Russia was in no position to contest the decision. However, the Kremlin never recognized Rumania's right to the territory.

[2] *Documents, op. cit.,* June 23-26, 1940, pp. 155-62.

the Soviet Government had never reconciled itself to the forcible seizure of Bessarabia by Rumania and this fact had been stated before the entire world many times by the USSR. "Now," said the note, "the military weakness of the USSR had become a thing of the past, and the present situation demands the speediest solution of outstanding issues inherited from the past." Therefore, the Soviet Government regarded it as necessary, timely, and in the interests of justice to begin immediate negotiations with Rumania regarding the return of Bessarabia to the Soviet Union. Furthermore, the note continued, "the restoration of Bessarabia is organically linked with the transfer to the Soviet Union of that part of Bucovina, the population of which in its overwhelming majority is bound with the Soviet Ukraine by unity of historic destinies as well as by unity of language and national composition." Moreover, such an act "would be all the more just in that the transfer would constitute—it is true only an insignificant degree—a means of compensation for the tremendous harm inflicted on the Soviet Union by twenty-two years of Rumanian domination in Bessarabia." And lastly, "The Government awaits the reply of the Royal Government of Rumania during the course of June 27." This note was handed to the Rumanian Minister at 10 P.M. on June 26.[3]

After a few hectic hours of deliberation, the Rumanians instructed their Minister in Moscow, Davidescu, to reply that the Royal Rumanian Government was "prepared to proceed immediately and in the broadest sense to a friendly discussion with common accord of all the proposals emanating from the Soviet Union", and for the USSR to designate the place and date for such a discussion. Molotov apparently designated that moment as the "date" and Moscow as the "place" for he then asked Davidescu if his government accepted the demands. The Minister replied in the affirmative. Molotov stated that on this basis he regarded the matter as settled. However, after a few hours deliberation within the Politburo, Molotov notified Davidescu that the Soviet Union demanded a more definite affirmative answer. He further insisted that within four days Rumania evacuate completely, including troops, all of Bessarabia and Northern Bucovina and that in so doing no damage be done to railroads, airdromes, public buildings, telegraph installations, etc. The Rumanian Government was given until noon of the following day, June 28, to make a satisfactory reply.

If during the next few hours Rumania entertained at all the idea of war to defend her borders, she received word from Germany which greatly discouraged any such notion. Ribbentrop informed Rumania

[3] *Moscow News*, July 3, 1940.

late in the morning of June 27 that "in order to avoid war between Rumania and the Soviet Union, we can only advise the Rumanian Government to yield to the Soviet Government's demand."[4] Thus, shortly before the time limit expired, Davidescu informed Molotov that Rumania accepted the Soviet demands. He asked only for an extension of time in which to carry out the evacuation. Molotov informed him that "several hours" could be granted "in case of necessity" but stated bluntly that during that afternoon (June 28), "Soviet troops will begin to cross the Rumanian frontier to occupy the cities of Chernovtsy, Kishinev, and Akkerman."[5]

Within two days the Red Army had "liberated" Bessarabia from the "Rumanian imperialist vultures" and at the same time had reunited the kindred Ukrainians with their ethnic homeland.[6] The entire operation was carried out with great speed by Red Army tanks, planes and parachutists in a manner which hardly suggested that the matter had been settled by "friendly discussion." By the first of July, the occupation was an accomplished fact; Bessarabia and Northern Bucovina were component parts of the USSR.

With the reacquisition of Bessarabia, Soviet Russia added 17,146 square miles and a 3,200,000 population to its ever-increasing total of land and people. With this could be included the roughly 2,300 square miles and 500,000 people of Northern Bucovina, never before a part of either Tsarist or Soviet Russia. It was an impressive total for only one week of action.

Germany, Soviet Russia's erstwhile partner, was as surprised as anyone. Schulenburg observed in a telegram to Berlin that "Some things are not as yet completely clear, as for instance the question as to why the Soviet Union just at this time proceeded or allegedly will yet proceed against a number of countries." He remarked that several of his diplomatic colleagues were of the opinion that the Soviets—"who are always well informed"—assumed the end of the war to be imminent. There would be reason to believe that all Soviet actions at this time (or any time) were inspired by the idea of expansion into voids where no effective resistance presented itself for one reason or another. As the Soviets saw it, the void in Bessarabia and Northern Bucovina was one of the immediate moment. In a matter of days, even hours, it would

---

[4] *Documents, op. cit.,* June 27, 1940, p. 163.

[5] *Moscow News,* July 3, 1940.

[6] The ethnic composition of Bessarabia, according to the Russian census of 1897 was 48% Rumanian (or Moldavian), and 28% Russian and Ukrainian. In 1930, Rumanian authorities reported 56% Rumanian (or Moldavian) and only 23% Russian or Ukrainian. Jews made up 12% of the Bessarabian population.

have ceased to exist and with it the opportunity to expand would, at best, be one of the far future.

In regard to Northern Bucovina, Schulenburg noted that prior to this time (June 1940), "There had never been any statement of Soviet claims to this region." The claim itself was based on the presumption that Bucovina had a Ukrainian population—but this fact was actually true only in the northern section, to which the Soviet Government had finally agreed to limit its demands. Undoubtedly, Soviet multi-national policy, and in particular Ukrainian nationalism, played an important part in this acquisition. If so, although it had gained for the USSR an immediate strategic and territorial advantage, Ukrainian nationalism was to prove a disadvantage in future relations with the Germans.

"I cannot get rid of the impression," commented Schulenburg, "that it was Ukrainian circles in the Kremlin who have advocated and put through the claim for cession of Northern Bucovina. On several occasions, as for instance during the negotiations regarding the German-Soviet border in Poland, a very strong Ukrainian influence in the Kremlin was evident. Herr Stalin told me personally at that time that he was prepared to make concessions north of the boundary line where it runs through White Russia, but this was impossible in the south where Ukrainians live." [7]

If such was the case, there is reason to believe that the multinational federal structure could promote dangerous opportunism on the part of a Soviet Union Republic which in turn might prove perilous to the existence of the USSR. For instance, Ukrainian expansion into Bucovina generated suspicion in German circles which doubtless hastened the eventual break between the Soviet Union and Germany. Hitler was provided with a justification for his supposition that Germany could not act decisively against England in the west for fear the USSR would once again move in the east. [8]

Hardly a week had passed after the new acquisitions before the

[7] *Documents, op. cit.*, July 11, 1940, pp. 164-65. The Ukrainian influence of which Schulenburg speaks was undoubtedly very strong in the Politburo. It consisted of Khrushchev, head of the Ukrainian Communist Party and a strong Ukrainian nationalist; Marshal Voroshilov, for many years head of the Red Army; Kaganovich, head of heavy industry and Vice-Premier of the Soviet Union; and the late Andrei Zhdanov, a native Ukrainian.

[8] In his dispatch to the German Foreign Office, July 11, 1940, Schulenburg stated that "The entire political interest here in Moscow . . . is on what will happen in relation to Turkey and Iran . . . excitement is extremely great. Both Ambassadors here assert that neither in Moscow nor in Ankara nor in Teheran have any demands been made up to present. However, it is certain that the situation is serious." *Ibid.*, July 11, 1940, pp. 164-5.

Moldavian Autonomous Soviet Republic proposed to the Supreme Soviet that it be given the status of a Union Republic. This was to be accomplished by combining Soviet Moldavia with those recently acquired areas of Bessarabia composed of predominantly Moldavian and Rumanian populations.[9] The remaining areas and Northern Bucovina were to be added to the Ukrainian Soviet Republic. This proposition became an accomplished fact on August 2, 1940, at the Seventh Session of the Supreme Soviet, when Moldavia became the thirteenth Union Republic of the USSR. Once again the multinational character of the federal constitution played an important part in the territorial seizures from Rumania. A new state was thus created in Eastern Europe; for Communist purposes and Russian purposes, ethnically similar to the one it bordered, Rumania; a state which could act with the force of the 190,000,000 population of the Soviet Union yet which would attempt to assume only the obligations and responsibilities of some 2,000,000 Moldavian Soviet citizens. The new Moldavian state would thereafter present itself as the true voice of all free Moldavians and Rumanians not under the yoke of capitalist imperialism, and would not rest content until these kindred souls were subjected to the freedom of the Soviet Union.

Strategically, the addition of these two regions was of great value. They formed the natural borderlands of the Russian plains, and, for purposes of defense, natural geographic features of considerable importance. Politically, these new areas provided additional territory in which Communist theory could be put into practice. Finally, the new conquest placed the Soviet Union in a stronger position to influence the affairs of Southeast Europe, a consideration of particular importance at that time.

For a considerable period of years, however, the voice of the USSR was one of compelled restraint. From that moment on, the Germans acted to consolidate and extend their power in the Balkans with almost the same nimble adroitness used by the Soviets in acquiring Bessarabia. Hitler was doubtless prodded into moving quickly and decisively by the mounting Soviet encroachment in the area. The 23,000,000 people

---

[9] According to Frank Lorimer (*The Population of the Soviet Union*, Geneva, League of Nations, 1945, p. 187), "Part of the Moldavian SSR, formerly a part of the Ukrainian SSR, was assigned to the newly formed Moldavian SSR, involving the political transfer of 310,000 persons. . . . The Moldavian SSR was formed by the major portion of Bessarabia (28,800 square kilometers with an estimated 2,100,000 persons) and part of the former Moldavian SSR (3,900 square kilometers with 310,000 persons). The remainder of the latter area, with a large Ukrainian population, remained within the Ukrainian SSR and was transferred to the Odessa District."

and approximately 165,000 square miles of territory that the USSR acquired during its first year of friendship with Nazi Germany was to grow no larger until the later days of the Second World War. Actually, these gains were to diminish to nothing when the glorious cooperation of the totalitarian giants came to an end the following summer. While the legality of the Russian seizures was assured by their incorporation into Soviet Republics, they nevertheless were the beginning of the end of a policy of lucrative neutrality perhaps unequaled in modern times.

CHAPTER 7

PLANS FOR AGGRANDIZEMENT

"When two thieves fall out, honest people gain."—Lenin, 1920.

Although the disintegration of the Nonaggression Pact and the Secret Protocols began when Soviet Russia struck in Bessarabia and Bucovina, the Nazi-Soviet relationship continued for almost a year longer. The only problem of immediate territorial concern to the Soviet Union, following the profitable summer of 1940, was a small strip of territory in the southwest corner of Lithuania which by terms of the secret agreement fell within the German sphere of influence. Much to the annoyance of the Reich, Red Army troops had occupied the area when they overran Lithuania. Consequently, Molotov, with a settlement in mind, summoned Schulenburg on July 13, 1940 and acknowledged that the Soviet obligation to cede the territory to Germany was incontestible, but stressed that "numerous difficulties" were involved in such an act. He said that Stalin hoped that Germany would not insist on the cession.[1]

Ribbentrop, in his reply, asked what *quid pro quo* the USSR proposed in exchange. The Kremlin immediately offered $3,860,000 in gold or goods in kind, but Germany signified the amount was unsatisfactory. There the matter rested until January 10, 1941, when a Secret Protocol was signed whereby the Soviet Union payed $7,500,000 in gold and thus assumed control of the territory in question.[2]

Of far greater concern than the small strip of Lithuanian territory, however, was the new relationship between Nazi Germany and Communist Russia. Soviet machinations in the Baltic and Balkans had stimulated feverish foreign office activity by Germany—all to the territorial, political, and economic disadvantage of the USSR. Germany seized and made unavailable to Soviet Lithuania, the port of Memel,

---

[1] Schulenburg to Foreign Office, *Documents, op. cit.,* July 13, 1940, p. 166.
[2] *Ibid.,* January 10, 1941, p. 267.

which, by a German dictated treaty of March 22, 1939, had been established as a Free Zone by Lithuania to facilitate the eventual return of
this area to the Third Reich. In that Memel was Lithuania's chief port,
the matter caused great resentment in the Narkomindel. Ribbentrop's
reasoning that the State of Lithuania no longer existed doubtless had
considerable basis in fact, but when he argued that the Russians controlled so many other Baltic ports that they did not need Memel, the
Kremlin was not disposed toward sympathy.

Nor were the Soviets enthusiastic about the German policy in the
Balkans which culminated in the so-called Vienna Award. This adjustment, arranged by Germany and Italy, effected a settlement of Hungarian and Bulgarian territorial claims against Rumania, in return
for which Germany and Italy guaranteed Rumania's new and dimin-
ished frontier against further aggression. The Soviets claimed that this
agreement violated the consultative clause of the Nonaggression Pact,
and inferred correctly that it was directed against USSR. Germany
retorted that it did not violate any mutual agreement between the two
countries, and that the act was a contribution to peace after the USSR
had initiated the Rumanian partition. Moreover, the Nazis maintained,
since Soviet interest had been satisfied by the cession of Northern
Bucovina and Bessarabia, there were no common interests and no
obligation to consult with the USSR.

No sooner had Soviet Russia adjusted itself to the Vienna Award
and the resulting German predominance in the Balkans, than Molotov
was informed casually on September 21, 1940, that German troops
were being moved through Finland to northern Norway. This, explained the Germans, was a purely technical matter and had no political
implications. Certain areas of northern Norway could be reached only
through Finland, and as a result the German Government had ex-
changed notes to this effect with the Finnish Government. "In view
of the purely technical communications aspect of the matter we naturally saw no reason expressly to notify the Soviet Government of it,"
was Schulenburg's explanation to an annoyed Molotov.*

The next blow to the Narkomindel was even less comforting.
Molotov was informed on September 26, 1940, that because of war-
mongering agitation in America, the Germans, Italians, and Japanese
had concluded a military alliance, but that this alliance was in no way
directed against the USSR. Molotov was not so sure. He immediately
asked for the text of the agreement and to discuss any secret protocols

*Ribbentrop to German Embassy in USSR, Oct. 2, 1940, *Documents, op. cit.*, pp.
201-03.

that might have been affixed. He was politely informed that the text had been published by the press and since the Three Power Agreement had not been directed against the USSR, there was no obligation to discuss the matter.[3]

Then, on October 17, 1940, came a letter from Ribbentrop to Stalin, reviewing events since August 1939, and pointing out the gains that had accrued to both parties from the Nazi-Soviet Pact. The letter intimated that it would be most desirable to establish more intimate relations between the USSR and the members of the Three Power Agreement and suggested that Molotov visit Berlin to formulate a common policy. The Soviet Government immediately accepted the invitation, and on November 12, 1940, Molotov was warmly welcomed in the German capital.

The conversations that followed were a climax to the grand friendship of the two totalitarian powers. The Soviet Union, however, did not realize this fact until late the following winter at a time too late to avert war. Molotov's meticulous and methodical mind, it turned out, was a decided detriment when dealing with the grandiose plans and ambitions of the Nazi Fuhrer.

The conversations between Hitler, Ribbentrop, and Molotov which followed were of great historical importance. The discussions revealed not only the vicious territorial ambitions of Nazi Germany—known to all and not soon forgotten—but also the equally predatory and ambitious aspirations of the Soviet Union—known to few and generally forgotten.

The first conversation of the Nazi-Soviet conclave was between Ribbentrop and Molotov. For his visitor's benefit, Ribbentrop reviewed the existing military situation to show that Britain was already beaten, and then stated that Hitler was anxious for an agreement on the spheres of influence of Germany, Russia, Italy, and Japan. Molotov's reply, in essence, was that he required a more precise definition of the respective spheres of influence, and that terms like "Greater East Asian Sphere" would have to be defined before the Soviet could discuss the matter of spheres in detail."[4]

Immediately following his conversation with Ribbentrop, Molotov conferred with Hitler. The Fuhrer began by explaining the reasons for many of the German actions which he thought were perhaps difficult for the Soviet Union to understand. The reason, explained Hitler,

[3] *Documents, op. cit.,* October 2, 1940, p. 201.
[4] Conversation between Ribbentrop and Molotov, *Ibid.,* November 12, 1940, pp. 217-25.

was that Germany was at war while Soviet Russia was not, and hence many German decisions and actions were often the result of events which could never be adequately foreseen. Neither the Soviets nor the Germans, Hitler continued, had realized all of their territorial wishes in the past nor would they realize all of them in the future, but if the two nations went along together they would both gain considerably more than if they worked against each other. Molotov agreed whole-heartedly. Hitler then outlined at length the emerging world situation and the place of both Soviet Russia and Nazi Germany in relation to it. In the coming world order, said Hitler, it would be mutually advantageous for Germany, Russia, Italy, and Japan to agree beforehand on definite spheres of interest so that joint territorial aims could be fully realized and best utilized without conflict.

Molotov replied that in general he could agree with Hitler's reasoning. However, the thing of particular importance to the Soviet Union, he said, was the meaning of the New Order in Europe and Asia, and what role the USSR was to be given in it. Moreover, there were issues to be clarified regarding Russia's Balkan and Black Sea interests with respect to Bulgaria, Rumania, and Turkey. It would be easier, Molotov pointed out, for the Russian Government to give specific replies to the questions raised by the Fuhrer if it could obtain the explanations just requested.

Hitler answered that the Tripartite Pact between Germany, Italy, and Japan was intended to regulate conditions in Europe, and consequently Germany was approaching Russia in order that she might express herself regarding areas of interest to her. He hoped that the discussion would be the first step in a comprehensive collaboration with due consideration for the problems of Western Europe which were to be settled between Germany and Italy, as well as for the issues of the Far East which were essentially the concern of Russia and Japan, but in which Germany offered her good offices as mediator.

Molotov replied that Soviet participation in the Tripartite Pact appeared to him entirely acceptable in principle, provided that Russia was to cooperate as a partner and not be merely an object. However, as he had just told Ribbentrop, he felt that precise definitions were necessary for the aims and significance of the Pact and for terms such as "Greater East Asian Sphere."

During his second discussion with Hitler the following day, Molotov opened with a complaint about the German use of Finland for transportation of troops to northern Norway. In this operation, the Russian commented, Germany had not fulfilled the German-Russian agreement nor the Secret Protocols. Obviously irritated, Hitler replied that in the Secret Protocol zones of influence and spheres of interest had been designated and distributed between Germany and Russia. In so far as it had been a question of actually taking possession, Germany had lived up to the agreements, which was not quite the case on the Russian side. "At any rate," said Hitler pointedly, "Germany had not occupied any territory that was within the Russian sphere of influence."[5]

In regard to Lithuania, continued Hitler, there was no doubt but that changes from the original German-Russian agreement were essentially due to Russian initiative. In any case, the district of Lublin was no compensation economically for Lithuania. The Germans had seen, however, that in the course of events a situation had arisen which necessitated revision of the original agreement. The same applied to Bucovina. Strictly speaking, said Hitler, Germany had declared herself disinterested only in Bessarabia; nevertheless, in this case too, revision of the agreement was in certain respects advantageous for the other partner.

In regard to Finland, he continued, Germany recognized that politically this country fell within the Russian sphere of influence. However, Germany had to consider two points: first, the delivery of nickel and lumber from Finland; and second, security against British action in the Baltic or in northern Norway. These were necessities of war, he concluded, and would not continue after hostilities ended.

Molotov stated that he agreed generally with the remarks of Hitler. However, Molotov remarked, if he were to draw up a balance sheet of the situation that resulted after the defeat of France, he would have to state that the German-Russian agreement had not been without influence upon the great German victories. Molotov insisted that the Soviet Government would not have refused to leave matters as provided in the original agreement, but at any rate, Germany, for its concession in Lithuania, had received compensation in Polish territory. Regarding Bucovina, Molotov admitted that this involved an additional territory not mentioned in the Secret Protocol. Russia had at first confined her demands to Northern Bucovina, but under the present circumstances Germany should understand the Russian interest in Southern Bucovina. The Soviet Government had been anxious to receive an answer to this question too, said Molotov, but Germany had instead guaranteed the entire territory of Rumania and had completely disregarded Russia's wishes in respect to Southern Bucovina.[6]

---

[5] *Documents, op. cit.,* November 13, 1940, p. 234.

[6] Southern Bucovina contained relatively few "kindred Ukrainians." The only

Hitler replied that it would mean a considerable concession on the part of Germany if even part of Bucovina were to be occupied by Russia. The former Austrian territories, Hitler reminded the Russian, fell within the German sphere of influence. The territories belonging to the Russian zone had been mentioned by name: Bessarabia, for example. To an objection by Molotov that the revisions with regard to the strip of Lithuanian territory and of Bucovina were not very important in comparison with the revision which Germany had undertaken elsewhere by military force, Hitler replied emphatically that "revision by force of arms" had not been the subject of the agreement at all.

If German-Russian collaboration was to show positive results in the future, Hitler warned, the Soviet Government would have to understand that Germany was engaged in a life and death struggle, which, at all events, she wanted to conclude successfully. The Soviet Union had to realize that, in the framework of any broader collaboration of the two countries, advantages of a quite grander scope were to be reached than the insignificant revisions which were then being discussed. Much larger successes could be achieved, said Hitler, provided that Russia did not pursue an aggressive policy in territories in which Germany was interested for the duration of the war. Future gains would be greater, he continued, the more Germany and Russia managed to fight back to back against the outside world, and would become smaller, the more the two countries faced each other breast to breast. In the first case, concluded Hitler, there was no power on earth that could oppose the two countries.

In reply, Molotov expressed agreement with Hitler's conclusions, but emphasized that in order to strengthen relations between the two countries secondary issues would first have to be resolved. Finland belonged among these issues. If Russia and Germany were in basic accord the issue could be solved without war, but neither German troops in Finland nor political demonstrations in that country against the Soviet-Russian Government could be tolerated.

Hitler responded that he knew nothing about demonstrations, but could assure Molotov that, if an agreement were made, German troops would appear in Finland no longer. He was particularly concerned, however, lest a conflict lead once again to the spread of hostilities in that area.

Molotov did not appear satisfied with Hitler's answer and con-

basis for Soviet possession would be the increased security aspect and the always present missionary aim of liberation from capitalist exploitation, etc. The territory, as mentioned above, had never before formed a part of Tsarist or Soviet Russia.

tinued to press the subject of Finland. Peace in the Baltic region, he repeatedly insisted, could be absolutely insured if perfect understanding were attained between Germany and Russia in the Finnish matter, but Russia did not like to postpone the realization of her wishes in this area. Asked by Hitler if Russia would declare war on the United States if the latter should intervene in a new Russo-Finnish war, Molotov stated that the question was not of present interest. Hitler replied that it would be too late for a decision when it became so.

On German initiative, the discussion then turned to "more important problems", as Hitler described them. After the conquest of England, Hitler revealed, the British Empire would be apportioned as a gigantic world-wide estate in bankruptcy of 40,000,000 square kilometers. All the countries which could possibly be interested in the bankrupt estate would have to stop all controversies among themselves and concern themselves exclusively with the partition of the British Empire. This applied to Germany, Vichy-France, Italy, Russia, and Japan. In this connection, Hitler went on, Germany did not want to annex France as the Russians appeared to assume.

Hitler expounded his grandiose plans at length. When he eventually stopped to hear Molotov's ideas, he was abruptly brought back to earth by the Russian's insistence upon talking of the Turkish problem, the question of Russian participation on the Danube Commission, Russia's dissatisfaction with the German guarantee of Rumanian borders, the Straits question, alteration of the Montreux Convention, and so forth. Somewhat disturbed, Hitler finally called attention to the late hour and the conversation was completed.

Later that evening, Molotov engaged in a final discussion with Ribbentrop. The German Foreign Minister outlined a broad division of the spheres of influence of Germany, Italy, Japan, and the USSR, and in addition specifically invited the Soviet to adhere to the Tripartite Pact. The actual agreement, said Ribbentrop, would be made public, but beyond that a confidential secret agreement would be concluded establishing the focal points in the territorial aspirations of the four countries. As for Germany, he remarked, apart from the territorial revisions to be made in Europe at the conclusion of the peace, her territorial aspirations centered in the Central African region. Japanese aspirations would still have to be clarified through diplomatic channels, but Ribbentrop thought that here too a delimitation could be found, possibly by fixing a line which would run south of the Japanese home islands and Manchukuo. Italy's territorial aspirations, aside from the European territorial revisions, centered in North and Northeast Africa. The focal points in the territorial aspirations of the Soviet Union, Ribbentrop went on, would presumably be centered south of the territory of the Soviet Union in the direction of the Indian Ocean. These agreements, Ribbentrop pointed out, could be supplemented by a second secret protocol, to be concluded between Germany, Italy, and the USSR. The second protocol could read that the three powers were agreed that it was in their common interest to release Turkey from her previous ties and win her progressively to political collaboration with them. The protocol would also provide cooperation whereby the three powers would jointly exert their influence to the end that the Montreux Straits Convention[7] would be replaced by another convention which would accord to the Soviet Union the unrestricted right of passage through the Straits for her warships at any time. All other powers, other than those of the Black Sea, Italy, and Germany, would renounce in principle the right of passage through the Straits for their warships.

Ribbentrop also inferred that Germany was ready and anxious to assist in bringing about better relations between the Soviet Union and Japan. The desire of the Japanese Government to come to a broad understanding with the USSR was known to him, said Ribbentrop. He was also of the opinion that if the nonaggression pact materialized, the Japanese would be prepared to settle all other issues in a generous manner. He was certain that Japan would be willing to recognize the Russian spheres of influence in Outer Mongolia and Sinkiang, provided an understanding with China was reached. An agreement could also be attained on possible Soviet aspirations in the direction of British India, on the condition that an understanding were achieved between the Soviet Government and the Tripartite Pact. Moreover, Ribbentrop told the attentive Molotov, the Japanese Government was disposed to meet Soviet wishes half-way in regard to the oil and coal concessions on Sakhalin Island, although it would first have to overcome resistance at home. This would be easier for the Japanese Government, of course, if a nonaggression pact were first concluded with the Soviet Union.

Molotov indicated his hope and conviction that Russia and Japan would now make more progress toward an understanding than before, but that the solution of the problem would require some time. As to Turkey, it was first necessary to reach an understanding on the Straits question. The Montreux Convention was worthless. In the course of history, said Molotov, Russia had often been attacked by way of the Straits and would have to insist on effective guarantees for her security.

7 See Chapter 12.

In Eastern Europe, he continued, the USSR was interested not only in Turkey, but Bulgaria, Rumania, and Hungary. Furthermore, the Soviet Union was especially anxious to know what the Axis contemplated in regard to Yugoslavia and Greece, and what the future German plans were in Poland. Also, was Germany still anxious to preserve Swedish neutrality?

Ribbentrop answered that German actions in the Balkans were motivated solely by wartime economic motives and the desire to keep England from disturbing the situation there. Germany had guaranteed Rumania's borders only to prevent a clash between Hungary and Rumania. Rumania, he pointed out, would never have ceded so much territory to Hungary if she had not in return received a guarantee against future dismemberment from Germany. All German actions in the Balkans, said Ribbentrop, stemmed from the war with England, and nothing else. Once peace was concluded, Germany's interest would be solely in the economic field. He insisted that there were no German territorial aspirations in the Balkans. However, the decisive and important question of these talks, Ribbentrop emphasized, was whether the Soviet Union was prepared to cooperate with Germany in the great liquidation of the British Empire. All other questions could easily be solved if the bigger question of spheres of influence was first settled.

Molotov replied that he quite approved of large-scale collaboration. He also concurred that a delimitation of the spheres of influence must be sought. However, concluded Molotov, definite solutions should be reached in the situations he had already mentioned before proceeding to new tasks. With that remark, the conversation came to a close. Molotov returned to Moscow the next day, November 14, 1940.[8]

A few days later in the Russian capital, Schulenburg presented the Narkomindel with a German draft of the proposed agreement between the Tripartite Powers and the Soviet Union. A good portion of the proposed text is particularly relevant.

"The Governments . . . of the Three Power Pact, Germany, Italy, and Japan on one side and the Government of the USSR on the other side, motivated by the desire to establish in their natural spheres of influence in Europe, Asia, and Africa, a new order serving the welfare of all peoples concerned and to create a firm and enduring foundation to their common labors toward this goal, have agreed upon the following:[9]

[8] Material on the German-Soviet Conversations was obtained from *Documents, op. cit.*, November 12-13, 1940. pp. 217-55.

[9] *Ibid.*, pp. 255-58.

"*Article I:* . . . The Soviet Union declares that it concurs in the aims of the

"SECRET PROTOCOL NUMBER ONE.

"1) Germany declares that, apart from the territorial revisions in Europe to be carried out at the conclusion of peace, her territorial aspirations center in the territories of Central Africa.

"2) Italy declares that, apart from the territorial revisions in Europe to be carried out at the conclusion of peace, her territorial aspirations center in the territories of Northern and Northeastern Africa.

"3) Japan declares that her territorial aspirations center in the area of Eastern Asia to the south of the Island Empire of Japan.

"4) *The Soviet Union declares that its territorial aspirations center south of the national territory of the Soviet Union in the direction of the Indian Ocean.*" (Author's italics.)

"SECRET PROTOCOL NUMBER TWO: TO BE CONCLUDED AMONG GERMANY, ITALY, AND THE SOVIET UNION.

"1) Germany, Italy, and the Soviet Union agree in the view that it is in their common interest to detach Turkey from her existing international commitments and progressively to win her over to political collaboration with themselves. They declare that they will pursue this aim in close consultation, in accordance with a common line of action which is still to be determined.

"2) Germany, Italy, and the Soviet Union declare their agreement to conclude, at a given time, a joint agreement with Turkey, wherein the Three Powers would recognize the extent of Turkey's possessions.

"3) Germany, Italy, and the Soviet Union will work in common toward the replacement of the Montreux Straits Convention now in force, by another convention. By this convention the Soviet Union would be granted the right of unrestricted passage of its navy through the Straits at any time, whereas all other Powers except the other Black Sea countries, but including Germany and Italy, would in prin-

---

Three Power Pact and is on its part determined to cooperate politically in this course with the Three Powers. . . .

"*Article II:* Germany, Italy, Japan, and the Soviet Union undertake to respect each other's natural spheres of influence. In so far as these spheres of interest come into contact with each other, they will constantly consult each other in an amicable way with regard to the problems arising therefrom.

"Germany, Italy, and Japan declare on their part that they recognize the present extent of the possessions of the Soviet Union and will respect it.

"*Article III:* [The Four Powers] undertake to join no combination of powers and to support no combination of powers which is directed against one of the Four Powers. [They] will assist each other in economic matters in every way and will supplement and extend the agreements existing among themselves.

"*Article IV:* The agreement shall take effect upon signature and shall continue for a period of ten years."

ciple renounce the right of passage through the Straits for their naval vessels. The passage of commercial vessels through the Straits would, of course, have to remain free in principle."[10]

After the Politburo had discussed, debated, and finally decided on the proposed Four Power Pact, a perhaps overconfident Molotov summoned Schulenburg to the Soviet Foreign Office. "The Soviet Government," he announced, "is prepared to accept the draft of the Four Power Pact outlined by the Reich Foreign Minister in the conversation of November 13 regarding political collaboration and reciprocal economic support *(unterstutzung)*, subject to the following conditions:

"1) Provided that the German troops are immediately withdrawn from Finland, which, under the compact of 1939, belongs to the Soviet Union's sphere of influence. At the same time the Soviet Union undertakes to ensure peaceful relations with Finland and to protect German economic interests in Finland (export of lumber and nickel).

"2) Provided that within the next few months the security of the Soviet Union in the Straits is assured by the conclusion of a mutual assistance pact between the Soviet Union and Bulgaria, which geographically is situated inside the security zone of the Black Sea boundaries of the Soviet Union, and by the establishment of a base for land and naval forces of the USSR within range of the Bosporus and the Dardanelles by means of a long-term lease.

"3) *Provided that the area south of Batum and Baku in the general direction of the Persian Gulf is recognized as the center of the aspirations of the Soviet Union.* (Author's italics)

"4) Provided that Japan renounces her rights to concessions for coal and oil in Northern Sakhalin.

"5) In accordance with the foregoing, the draft of the protocol concerning the delimitation of the spheres of influence as outlined by the Reich Foreign Minister would have to be amended so as to stipulate *the focal point of the aspirations of the Soviet Union is south of Batum and Baku in the general direction of the Persian Gulf."* (Author's italics.)

"Likewise, the draft of the protocol or agreement between Germany, Italy, and the Soviet Union with respect to Turkey should be amended so as to guarantee a base for light naval and land forces of the USSR on the Bosporus and the Dardanelles by means of a long term lease, including—in case Turkey declares herself willing to join the Four Power Pact—a guarantee of the independence and of the territory of Turkey by the three countries named.

[10] *Documents, op. cit.,* November 15, 1940, p. 255.

"This protocol should provide that in case Turkey refuses to join the Four Powers, Germany, Italy, and the Soviet Union agree to work out and to carry through the required military and diplomatic measures, and a separate agreement to this effect should be concluded.

"Furthermore there should be agreement upon:

"(a) a third secret protocol between Germany and the Soviet Union concerning Finland (See Point 1 above).

"(b) a fourth secret protocol between Japan and the Soviet Union concerning the renunciation by Japan of the oil and coal concession in Northern Sakhalin (in return for an adequate compensation).

"(c) a fifth secret protocol between Germany, the Soviet Union, and Italy, recognizing that Bulgaria is geographically located inside the security zone of the Black Sea boundaries of the Soviet Union and that it is therefore a political necessity that a mutual assistance pact be concluded between the Soviet Union and Bulgaria, which in no way shall affect the internal regime of Bulgaria, her sovereignty or independence."[11]

It hardly need be said that this document is an incriminating exposition of Soviet territorial ambitions. The amazing thing is the price demanded by Soviet Russia for her continued neutrality. It would appear at first glance that the demands of the USSR were based upon equal participation with Germany, Italy and Japan in the New Order's design for conquest. Yet the Soviet Union was a neutral nation, and was demanding, as the price of her continued neutrality, Finland, Bulgaria, a predominant role in the Black Sea, control of the Straits, all of the area south of Batum and Baku, and strategic and economic concessions from Japan.

Hitler and Ribbentrop, of course, had attempted to persuade Molotov to steer Soviet territorial ambitions toward the Middle and Far East and away from Europe.

In fact, for Soviet neutrality, Nazi Germany had offered—and had been willing to concede at the outset—generally all that the Kremlin demanded except Bulgaria and Finland. Germany was willing to concede that Finland fell within Russia's sphere in principle only. From the tone of Molotov's remarks, however, the Soviets appeared particularly anxious to complete the earlier war and consolidate Finland solidly within their political if not their territorial sphere of control. But from the German standpoint, a renewal of hostilities in the Baltic area could very possibly have resulted in a large-scale conflict. If the Soviet Union was perhaps short-sighted about this dangerous possi-

[11] *Documents, op. cit.,* November 26, 1940, p. 258.

bility, Nazi Germany was not; Hitler was obviously concerned lest the United States, as well as Sweden participate in a new Russo Finnish War. Consequently, the Soviet demand for freedom of action against Finland was completely unacceptable to the German leaders.[12]

In regard to Bulgaria, it is evident that the USSR, frustrated by German strategy in Rumania, was anxious to improve its strategic position and eventually its territorial acquisitions in the Balkans. In spite of Russia's assertion that a mutual assistance pact would "in no way affect the internal regime of Bulgaria, her sovereignty, or independence", it would have been exceedingly difficult for an equally ruthless Germany, in view of Soviet violation of similar guarantees to the Baltic States and Finland, to assume that the Politburo would respect such a pledge for long.

There is also some doubt that Germany was willing to go to war with Turkey, as the Soviets had indirectly suggested, in the event Turkey did not agree to adjustment of the Straits question. Moreover, if Russian aims in regard to Turkey and the Straits had been realized, the Black Sea would have become little more than a Soviet lake, and the USSR would have assumed an increasingly important role in the Mediterranean.

Both the tone of Molotov's conversation and the presumptuous conditions attached to the proposed Four Power Pact were undoubtedly very annoying to German leaders. While Nazi Germany won the battles, Communist Russia shared the spoils. A misinformed, overconfident Soviet regime had overplayed its hand. This fact became evident less than a month later, on December 18, 1940, when Hitler decided that his neutral but omnivorous ally could be neither trusted nor purchased in the east. On this day, the Fuhrer informed the German High Command of "Operation Barbarossa", a tactical plan "to crush Soviet Russia in a quick campaign" even before the conclusion of war with England.[13]

From that moment on, relations between the two totalitarian giants continued to grow cooler and cooler. The Nazis, increasingly disdainful of the wishes of the Kremlin, occupied Bulgaria, invaded Greece, and overran Yugoslavia. The only consolation for Soviet diplomacy was the conclusion of a Neutrality Pact with Japan on April 13, 1941, an agreement later to be discarded when the Soviet Union attacked Japan a few

---

[12] Hitler's preoccupation with Finland had deeper roots. He never lost sight of his original program in *Mein Kampf*, which could not be realized without a war against the USSR.

[13] *Documents, op. cit.,* December 18, 1940, p. 260.

hours before the end of World War II in the Pacific. But the Japanese-Soviet Pact did not improve relations with Germany. On May 7, it was reported that Stalin had replaced Molotov as Chairman of the Council of Peoples Commissars, the highest position in the Soviet Government. Schulenburg informed Berlin that the change was officially explained as the pressure of work on Molotov, but that actually it meant a considerable abridgement of his former authority. Schulenburg calculated that the shift had been occasioned by the "recent mistakes in foreign policy which led to a cooling off of German-Soviet relations, the creation and preservation of which Stalin had consciously striven, while Molotov's own initiative often expended itself in an obstinate defense of individual issues." However, the situation by that time had developed far beyond a point where a change in Kremlin policy could have appreciably altered the future course of events. From then on, border incidents became increasingly common, and in spite of a decided effort on the part of the Soviet Government to preserve its lucrative neutrality, German troops crossed the Russian frontier June 23, 1941.

The territory gained in connivance with the equally presumptuous and ambitious Nazis was to be lost even quicker than it had been gained. The process of recovering the lost territories was expensive and prolonged. Some four years later the victorious Red Army once again asserted the right of the Russian Communists to the 1940 conquests—all gained, it should forever be remembered, in cooperation with their one-time Nazi ally.

CHAPTER 8

YALTA AND POTSDAM DECISIONS—POLAND AND GERMANY

"La raison du plus fort est toujours la meilleure."—La Fontaine, "Fables."

Even when it faced near defeat at the hands of the Nazi armies, the Soviet Union was concerned with the legalization and permanent confirmation of its 1940 territorial aggrandizement. And even when aid and assistance were immediately offered to the former Nazi ally by a hard-pressed Britain, the USSR was more concerned with verifying its earlier territorial seizures.[1] Nor was this concern subsequently forgotten by the Soviet Government. In the darkest moments of the war, the Kremlin continued to push for recognition of these seizures by Britain and the U. S.[2] And in the end, although it never succeeded in fully legalizing its ruthless acquisition of the Baltic republics, the Soviet nevertheless, by force of arms and successful diplomacy, legitimatized the Polish, Finnish, and Rumanian conquests and much more besides.

The most significant recognition of Russian territorial aims came at the Yalta conference in January 1945. It is of course difficult in retrospect to appreciate fully the complex situation confronting Roosevelt and Churchill as they faced Stalin at this meeting. But wittingly or unwittingly, they acted in collusion wtih him in the dismemberment not only of their wartime enemies, Germany and Japan, but also of their wartime allies, Poland and China. The territorial decisions at Yalta were a great victory for the Soviet Union.

Although the Polish question took considerable time at the conference, the decision on Poland's boundaries did not. An insistent Stalin was completely successful in his aims. On the eastern frontier he had little trouble in securing his wishes regarding the Russo-Polish border. Roosevelt, from the beginning, had agreed that the new border should

[1] Robert E. Sherwood, *Roosevelt and Hopkins, An Intimate History,* (New York, 1948), pp. 309-11.

[2] *Ibid.,* pp. 401; 451.

generally follow the so-called Curzon Line.[3] He felt, however, that it would be advisable to adjust the southern end of the line so that the city of Lwow with a portion of the nearby oilfields and most of Eastern Galicia (never Russian historically, but largely Ukrainian ethnically) should fall within Polish territory.[4] Churchill was even more generous than Roosevelt with the territory of his Polish ally—territory which Britain had presumably gone to war to defend in 1939. He supported the occupation of Lwow and Eastern Galicia by the USSR. The claim of the Soviet Union, he said, "is one not founded on force but upon right."[5] Be that as it may, Stalin professed at first not to be satisfied. But in the end, a line generally similar to the Curzon demarcation including Lwow and Eastern Galicia as part of the Soviet Ukraine was accepted as the Russo-Polish frontier.

To compensate Poland for this territory surrendered in the east, Stalin suggested that the Poles be given German territory in the west. "I am in favor of extending the Polish frontier to the Neisse River," he said.[6] Churchill and Roosevelt could not completely agree to this suggestion. Nevertheless, after lengthy discussion with Stalin, they arrived at a fairly definite compromise generally favorable to the Soviet Union. "The three heads of government," they announced, "consider that the eastern frontier of Poland should follow the Curzon Line with digressions from it in some regions of five to eight kilometers in favor of

[3] The Curzon Line was a provisional Eastern frontier for Poland drawn at the instance of Lord Curzon, British Foreign Minister, by the Allied Supreme Council in 1919. It excluded from the Polish State territories inhabited mainly by non-Polish populations—for the most part Ukrainians, White Russians, and Lithuanians. The Poles, however, ignored the decision and shortly thereafter overran Russian territories inhabited largely by Ukrainians and White Russians.

[4] In October, 1918, the Poles in Galicia renounced allegiance to Austria and claimed all Galicia for the new Polish State. The Ruthenians or Ukrainians, however, who comprised a large part of the area's population, claimed the right of self-determination and in November, 1918, formed a government in the city of Lwow. Shortly thereafter, the Poles forced this regime to retire and the area became one of conflict for several months. In May 1919, the Allied Supreme Council assigned Western Galicia to Poland, and in June gave Eastern Galicia the right of self-determination although authorizing continued Polish occupation. In December 1919, it announced that Eastern Galicia would be granted autonomy under a Polish protectorate for 25 years, after which the League of Nations was to decide on its future. Poland, however, treated the area as an integral part of its territory and it was recognized as such by the Council of Ambassadors on March 14, 1923. Following the partition of Poland in 1939, the area was appropriated by Germany.

[5] James F. Byrnes, *Speaking Frankly*, (New York, 1947), p. 29.

[6] *Ibid.*, p. 30. In demanding territory in addition to the Curzon Line, Stalin said, "Now some people want that we should be less Russian than Curzon was or Clemenceau was. You should drive us into shame."

Poland. They recognize that Poland must receive substantial accessions of territory in the north and west. They feel that the opinion of the new Polish Provisional Government of National Unity should be sought in due course on the extent of these accessions and that the final delimitation of the western frontier of Poland should thereafter await the peace conference."[7]

The "Polish Provisional Government of National Unity", mentioned by the Big Three in this protocol, was another compromise arrived at in conjunction with the boundary settlement. It sought to combine the Polish Government-in-Exile, which functioned in London, with the National Council of Poland, formed in Moscow and operated in Lublin, into a governing body for Soviet-occupied Poland. The decision arrived at by the three nations was that the Soviet-controlled Lublin regime should be "reorganized on a broader democratic basis with the inclusion of democratic leaders from Poland itself and from Poles abroad." The new government, said the conference communiqué, would be called the "Polish Provisional Government of National Unity." Moreover, according to the Yalta decisions, this new ruling group was pledged to hold free elections as soon as possible on the basis of universal suffrage and secret ballot. As it worked out, "as soon as possible" meant roughly eighteen months, and "free elections" meant "free" in the Soviet sense of the word. Furthermore, after Moscow had selected certain acceptable Poles from the London group for the Unity regime, several other members of this same London Government were accused and condemned as traitors by the USSR.

The background of these events dated from the reluctant entry of the Soviet Union into the war. It revealed once again various methods and techniques of Soviet territorial aggrandizement. Some five weeks after the German Army advanced across the Soviet frontier in 1941, an agreement was effected between the Polish Government in London and the USSR. By its terms the USSR recognized "the Soviet-German Treaties of 1939 regarding territorial changes in Poland as having lost their validity."[8] This one sentence meant that the Soviet Government therewith invalidated its actions of September 1939. In fact, it renounced its voracious territorial seizure or "liberation" of the Polish

[7] In his book *The Great Challenge* (London, 1947), Louis Fischer suggests that Roosevelt and Churchill were forced to concede territory to Russia at Yalta for fear that the USSR would negotiate a separate peace with Germany. He cites several incidents to prove his thesis and points out that the USSR never adhered to the "unconditional surrender" doctrine promulgated by Roosevelt and Churchill at Casablanca. (See pp. 257-62.)

[8] Agreement between the USSR and Poland, July 30, 1941.

Ukraine and Polish Byelorussia, and restored these areas in their entirety to the Polish Government in London, which it simultaneously recognized as the legal government of Poland. In addition, it annulled the results of the Soviet conducted 1939 plebiscite in which the USSR had alleged that better than ninety per cent of the voters of these areas had approved the Communist seizure.

However, on April 25, 1943, the outcome of the war looked considerably different than it had in 1942, and the Politburo abruptly reversed its earlier action. The Polish Government in London was notified that the Soviet Union had decided to "interrupt relations", ostensibly because the London Poles had insisted on conducting an investigation into the purported murder by the Russians of certain Polish officers near the city of Smolensk. The Soviet representatives insisted that the whole incident was the work of Nazi propaganda and had no basis of fact. These Poles, the Kremlin maintained, had actually been murdered by the Nazis. Whatever the case, it at least provided a cause whereby the Soviet Union could break relations with the Polish Government. At the same time, the USSR reasserted the claims to the Polish Western Ukraine and Polish Byelorussia which it had renounced as invalid twenty-one months earlier.[9]

Shortly thereafter, Moscow became politically aware of the "Congress of the Union of Polish Patriots in the USSR", which as far as the Soviets were concerned represented the real voice of the Polish people. The Kremlin then began to refer to the London Polish Government as the "emigré" group and inferred that it had no basis of popular support.[10]

On January 11, 1944 a Tass communiqué announced that the "Soviet Constitution has defined the Soviet-Polish frontier in accordance with the will of the population of Western Ukraine and Western Byelorussia, expressed in a plebiscite which was carried out on a broad democratic basis in 1939. On that occasion," it continued, "the territories of the Western Ukraine entered the Soviet Ukraine, while the territories of Western Byelorussia entered Soviet Byelorussia. The injustice permitted by the Riga Treaty of 1921 which was imposed upon the Soviet Union, in regard to the Ukrainians inhabiting Western Ukraine and the Byelorussians inhabiting Western Byelorussia, was in

[9] Note of the Soviet Government to the Polish Government, April 25, 1943.

[10] Address of the Congress of the Union of Polish Patriots of the USSR to J. V. Stalin, June 17, 1943; Reply by Stalin June 17, 1943; *Soviet Foreign Policy During the Patriotic War. Documents and Materials*, Vol. 1, June 22, 1941-December 31, 1943 (London 1944), translated by Andrew Rothstein.

this way rectified." With a show of righteous justification the Soviet declared that the entry of these territories into the USSR "not only did not infringe the interests of Poland, but, on the contrary, created a reliable basis for solid and permanent friendship between the Polish people and its neighbors, the Ukrainian, Byelorussian and Russian peoples." Poland should be reborn, asserted the Soviet Government, "not by the seizure of Ukrainian and Byelorussian lands, but by the restoration of lands belonging to her from time immemorial and wrested from Poland by the Germans." It then recommended that the new border "pass approximately along the so-called Curzon line" with modifications in favor of Poland where predominantly Polish populations formed a majority.

By summer 1944, the Red Army was advancing across Poland in pursuit of the retreating Germans. On July 26 the Narkomindel issued an important announcement: "The Soviet troops have entered Poland filled with one resolution—to crush the enemy German armies and to help the Polish people in its liberation from the yoke of the German invaders, and in the restoration of an independent, strong and democratic Poland." Moreover, "it has decided in view of this to conclude with the Polish Committee of National Liberation [established in Moscow] an agreement on relations between the Soviet Command and the Polish Administration. The Soviet Government states that it does not pursue the aim of acquiring any part of Polish territory or of changing the social order in Poland. . . . the brother peoples of the USSR and Poland . . . will lay durable foundations for friendly Soviet-Polish collaboration."[11]

By concluding an agreement with the Polish Liberation Committee, the Soviet Government recognized that group as the legally constituted government of Poland. To give a measure of legality to this procedure and at the same time to give the impression that Byelorussia, the Ukraine, and Lithuania were also actually sovereign nations,[12] a series of agreements were subsequently negotiated and signed by these Soviets on the one hand and the Polish Liberation Committee on the other. The character of the Polish group can be readily understood by statements it issued periodically through Tass, the Russian news agency: "Long Live the Great Stalin!" "Long Live the Alliance of Freedom-

11 Statement by the People's Commissariat for Foreign Affairs of the USSR, July 26, 1944.

12 In accordance with a Soviet Constitutional change of February 1, 1944, Soviet Republics were given the right to conclude treaties and carry on diplomatic relations with foreign governments.

Loving Peoples Fighting the Bloody Hitler!" "Friendship Between Our Polish People and the Brother Russian and Ukrainian Peoples."[13]

This then, was the government which Roosevelt and Churchill sought unsuccessfully to reconcile with the Polish Government in London. In the final analysis it was this same Soviet-created regime which formed the nucleus of Yalta compromise "Unity Government", and later the government which emerged victorious from the "free elections" of 1946.

In many respects the Soviet methods used in Poland during World War II were similar to those of the Soviet-Polish War following World War I. In both cases, Moscow established subservient puppet regimes which accompanied the Red Army as it moved across Poland. In World War II, however, the Red Army was considerably stronger and therefore the puppet regime survived and later became the legal government of Poland. This particular technique had been characteristic of several previous attempted territorial grabs by the USSR, but until the time of Poland its successes had been few. It was obvious that the success or failure of such methods rested largely on the strength of the Red Army.

The manner in which the Soviet Union withdrew recognition from the Polish Government in London was similar in some respects to Narkomindel action in withdrawing recognition from the Finnish Government in Helsinki in 1939. In the case of Finland, however, the Soviet was forced to discard its puppet government when circumstances made it necessary to conclude peace hurriedly with the legitimate government in Helsinki, the government that actually controlled Finnish soil. In the case of Poland, which had ceased to exist as a state in 1939, the USSR, after its entry into the war in 1941, established relations with the exile Polish Government in London. The London regime of course controlled no territory in that initially, 1939, Polish soil was either Sovietized or Nazified, and subsequently, 1941, it was over-run by the German Army. When the Soviets subsequently lost their section of partitioned Poland to the German Army, the Narkomindel consented to return to the London Poles all areas seized by the USSR in 1939, thereby displaying great generosity with territory at that time controlled by the Germans. Later, when it was evident that the Red Army would soon regain the areas lost to the German Army plus much more besides, the USSR found that its relations with the rather independent London Poles—a bourgeois government—and its promises in

13 Statement by representatives of the National Council of Poland, Tass dispatch, June 14, 1944.

regard to Polish territory were incompatible with the basic intentions and new strength of Soviet Russia. The Narkomindel therefore manufactured an incident and discarded the landless London Polish Government. Immediately thereafter, the Russians formed a Polish puppet regime in Moscow. Then, when the victorious Red Army swept across Poland, the Moscow Poles were established as the government on Polish soil, supported on the scene by the Red Army and abroad by the USSR. If any moral can be derived from these events, it is the cynical observation of La Fontaine that "The reason of the strongest is always the best."

With all these harsh facts presumably in mind, the British and American negotiators at Potsdam nevertheless agreed to the territorial revisions, demanded by the USSR. Stalin's suggestion that Poland be compensated in the west for Soviet seizures in the east was conditionally agreed to by both the U. S. and Britain. The only face-saving condition that the Anglo-Saxons were able to advance explaining the award of approximately 40,000 square miles to the Soviet-created Polish Government was that "The three heads of Government reaffirm their opinion that the final delimitation of the western frontier should await the peace settlement." But, pending the final determination, it was agreed that "the former German territories east of a line running from the Baltic Sea immediately west from Swinemuende, and thence along the Oder River to the confluence of the western Neisse River and along the western Neisse to the Czechoslovak frontier, including that portion of East Prussia not placed under the administration of the USSR . . . and including the area of the former free city of Danzig, shall be under the administration of the Polish State and for such purposes should not be considered as part of the Soviet zone of occupation in Germany."

Although by Western interpretation ownership was not therein implied, there are strong indications that in the Soviet and Polish versions, the words administration and ownership appear to be nearly synonomous. In all but name, these areas are now almost as much a part of Poland as is the district of Warsaw. Moreover, in that the U. S. and Britain had agreed to support this change at the Peace Conference, there was apparently little need for restraint on the part of the Poles in their future plans of territorial development.

On the eastern frontier, the USSR legalized its Ukrainian and White Russian seizures by an agreement with the new Polish Government.[14] The Russo-Polish frontier, as previously agreed at Yalta

---

[14] Soviet-Polish Treaty, signed August 16, 1945.

and Potsdam, followed generally the Curzon Line with small deviations conceded additionally to Poland. The nearly 69,000 square miles of territory seized by secret agreement with Hitler in 1939 were therefore made a legitimate Soviet acquisition. Moreover, this grand seizure included Eastern Galicia, not actually a part of Russia since the fourteenth century.[15]

The ethnological justification of Soviet aggrandizement had been supported by Roosevelt and by Churchill, who had said that the claim of the USSR was not founded on force but upon right.[16] Values had evidently changed. These were the same Western statesmen who a few years earlier had condemned and later gone to war at least partly because of Hitler's aggression on behalf of ethnic German minorities in Czechoslovakia, Austria, and elsewhere.

In addition to confirming the accession to the USSR of Polish lands gained through joint aggression with the Nazis in 1939, Article Five of the Potsdam Agreements stated that "The conference examined a proposal by the Soviet Government to the effect that, pending final determination of territorial questions at the peace settlement, the section of the western frontier of the USSR which is adjacent to the Baltic Sea should pass from a point on the eastern shore of the Bay of Danzig to the east, north of Braunsberg-Goldap to the meeting point of the frontiers of Lithuania, the Polish Republic and East Prussia. The conference has agreed in principle to the proposal of the Soviet Government concerning the ultimate transfer to the Soviet Union of the city of Koenigsberg and the area adjacent to it as described above." Lastly, "The President of the United States and the Prime Minister of Great Britain have declared that they will support the proposal of the conference at the forthcoming peace settlement."

To the victor went the spoils. Once again, the U.S. and Britain approved Soviet aggrandizement, but this time there was neither an historic nor ethnic basis for the Russian seizure. One way or another, however, the new territory was a strategic addition on the shores of the Baltic and increased the Soviet claim to pre-eminence on that sea. It provided additional security for the Soviet Baltic republics which, in their turn, had provided additional security for Leningrad. Furthermore, the acquisition of another ice-free port furnished assurance that Russia would have access to the open seas through the Baltic; more-

15 The area was occupied by Tsarist troops for a short while during World War I.
16 For that matter, the idea was also supported by Atlee, Eden, Bevin, Truman, Vandenberg, etc.—the leaders of the major parties in the U.S. and Britain.

over, the port of Koenigsberg could also serve as a naval base for the expanding Red Fleet.

On the other hand, the close relationship between the Moscow Government and the Warsaw Government, actually extended Soviet control of the Baltic to Stettin, in Polish-occupied Germany. To the east, the sections of Byelorussia and the Ukraine ceded to the USSR by the Poles gave the Russians control of the north and south approaches to the Pripet Marshes. To the south, the acquisitions from Poland established a common border with Czechoslovakia.

The idea of establishing common borders was a relatively new technique used for the purpose of exerting greater control on the policies of Soviet satellites, and was developed as much as possible in the postwar territorial adjustments. As for Communist theory, the Kremlin could consider the conquered areas legally free from imperialist exploitation and fully exposed to the consequences of collectivism—all, interestingly enough, with the consent of the bourgeois democracies. Furthermore, the Soviets could be quite sure of the future policies of their Polish brothers. The government of the new Poland was created in Moscow and would doubtless be at the mercy of Moscow. Officially, the two nations in all probability would work side by side for the advancement of collective democracy.

These then were the Soviet acquisitions approved by Yalta and Potsdam in the west. But they were far from all of the postwar territorial compensation granted to the Soviet Union. The Big Three were even more generous to Russia in the Far East, both with an enemy, Japan, and an ally, China.

CHAPTER 9

YALTA AND POTSDAM DECISIONS AND JAPAN

"I know you lawyers can with ease,
Twist words and meanings as you please."
—John Gay, *"Fables,"* 1727.

There were doubtless good reasons for the decisions of Roosevelt and Churchill at Yalta. Both men were aware that victory in the Pacific might cost hundreds of thousands of lives. Both men had just witnessed a murderous German counter-offensive on the western front. And both men were yet not fully aware of the potentialities of atomic destruction. Under these circumstances, they knew that the price of victory would be considerably less in human lives and that the Pacific War would end sooner if Russia were a participant. But Generalissimo Stalin was equally aware of these considerations. And he knew that he could demand and receive large territorial compensation for the services of the Red Army in the Far East. At Yalta he made good those demands.

The tragedy of compensating Soviet Russia was that the western allies gave considerably more than they were to possess in victory. While the British and Americans were at least within their so-called rights as victors when they agreed to award territory from the Empire of Japan to the USSR, they were contradicting their professed principles when they awarded the territory of their mutual ally, China, to the Soviet Union. Such demands for territory were not of course beyond the principles of the Soviet Union, but the fact that a supposedly high-principled Britain and the United States acted in concert with Soviet Russia toward the dismemberment of China in a black mark not soon erased.

The infamous secret agreement pledging the usurpation of Chinese authority as a compensation for Soviet promises to wage war on Japan was consummated during the final hours of the Yalta Conference. "The leaders of the three great powers," it said, "have agreed that two or three months after Germany has surrendered and the war in Europe has terminated, the Soviet Union shall enter into the war against Japan on the side of the Allies on condition that:

"1) The status quo in Outer Mongolia shall be preserved.*

"2) The former rights of Russia violated by the treacherous attack of Japan in 1904 shall be restored, viz:

"(a) The southern part of Sakhalin as well as the islands adjacent to it shall be returned to the Soviet Union;

"(b) The commercial port of Dairen shall be internationalized, the pre-eminent interests of the Soviet Union in this port being safe guarded, and the lease of Port Arthur as a naval base of the USSR restored;*

"(c) The Chinese Eastern Railroad and the South Manchurian Railroad which provide an outlet to Dairen, shall be jointly operated by establishment of a joint Soviet Chinese company, it being understood that the pre-eminent interests of the Soviet Union shall be safeguarded and that China shall receive full sovereignty in Manchuria.*

"3) The Kurile Islands shall be handed over to the Soviet Union."

To save this agreement from being completely odious, the following phrase was inserted: "It is understood that the agreement concerning Outer Mongolia and the ports and railroads referred to above will require concurrence of Generalissimo Chiang Kai-shek."

But the sentence following stated: "The President will take measures in order to obtain this concurrence on advice from Marshall Stalin." This statement assured the agreement of Chiang. The fact that the two most powerful nations on earth were to exert pressure on the Chinese Nationalists to accept the proposals was strong indication that they would be accepted. If there were still the slightest question, however, the agreement further specified that "The heads of the three governments have agreed that these claims of the Soviet Union shall be unquestionably fulfilled after Japan has been defeated."

There was only one condition for the Soviet Union to fulfill: namely, that it express "its readiness to conclude with the National Government of China a pact of friendship and alliance between the USSR and China in order to render assistance to China with its armed forces for the purpose of liberating China from the Japanese yoke." This condition was hardly an obligation. As evidenced by the pacts concluded in Europe, it was a distinct advantage to the foreign policy aims of the Soviet Union to conclude such an agreement.

The months following the Yalta Conference witnessed the final

*See Chapter 10.

victory of the Allied Powers in Europe. They also witnessed the untimely death of Franklin Roosevelt, the defeat of Winston Churchill as Prime Minister of Great Britain, and violations of the Yalta Agreements by the USSR in Poland and the Balkans. When the three powers met again at Potsdam in the summer of 1945, the war situation had changed greatly. The armed forces of the United States had battled to within a few hundred miles of the Japanese home islands and were preparing for a final assault the coming November. The United States, meanwhile, with the aid and assistance of the world's great scientists and its own mastery of production, had finally produced and detonated an atomic bomb. There was therefore little enthusiasm by the western powers at Potsdam for Soviet participation in the Pacific War. The agreement, however, had been made, and the U. S. and Britain were apparently in no position other than to carry out its provisions.

On the other hand, the Soviet Union had not reached an agreement with the Chinese Nationalist Government by the time of Potsdam nor did it appear that the Soviet Union was prepared to participate in the Pacific War in accordance with the pledges given at Yalta. Moscow had evidently planned on a longer war and was at the time making strong territorial demands on China in addition to those areas already promised Stalin at Yalta. Molotov showed visible concern when he learned that the Potsdam Declaration, backed up by the atomic bomb, might end the war before his country could join in the victory and thus share the spoils.

On July 29, 1945, Molotov told Byrnes that he was searching for an immediate pretext for his government to use in declaring war on Japan. He suggested that all of the Allied Powers address a formal request to the USSR for its entry into the war. Byrnes, however, was fully cognizant that Russia and Japan had a neutrality pact with nearly a year to run. He did not believe, he said, "that the United States Government should be placed in the position of asking another government to violate its agreement without good and sufficient reason."[1]

Byrnes' position at first gives the impression that the U.S. would not be party to a violation of an international agreement. The impression is misleading. Byrnes stated that he and another high official of the State Department, Ben Cohen, "spent hours" trying to concoct a valid reason which would enable the Soviet to evade the obligations of the neutrality pact and to satisfy Molotov's request. In one breath, it would appear, Byrnes did not believe that the U.S. should be party to a violation of an international agreement without good reason, and

[1] Byrnes, *op. cit.*, p. 205.

in the next breath he "spent hours" concocting such a reason to justify Soviet participation in the Pacific war.

The Byrnes-Cohen pretext was presented to the USSR in a letter from President Truman to Stalin. It first mentioned the Moscow Declaration of October 30, 1943, signed by the USSR, the United States, the United Kingdom, and China. This document declared that "for the purpose of maintaining international peace and security pending the re-establishment of law and order and inauguration of a system of general security, they will consult with one another and as occasion requires with other members of the United Nations with a view to joint action on behalf of the community of nations." The letter then mentioned that, according to Article 106 of the proposed United Nations Charter, the four powers would continue to act on the basis of the Moscow Declaration until the Charter came into force. Furthermore, Article 103 provided that "in the event of a conflict between the obligations of the Members of the United Nations under the present Charter and their obligations under any other international agreement, their obligations under the present Charter shall prevail." In conclusion the letter of President Truman pointed out that although "the Charter has not been formally ratified, at San Francisco it was agreed to by the Representative of the USSR, and the Soviet Government will be one of the permanent members of the Security Council . . . under terms of the Moscow Declaration and the provisions of the Charter, above-referred to, it would be proper for the Soviet Union to indicate its willingness to consult and co-operate with other great powers now at war with Japan with a view to joint action on behalf of the community of nations to maintain peace and security."[2]

So satisfactory was the Byrnes-Cohen approach that Stalin expressed great appreciation to President Truman for the communication. And Byrnes himself reluctantly admitted that his reasoning would doubtless facilitate Soviet historians to justify the Soviet declaration of war on Japan.[3]

On the day the second atomic bomb was dropped on Nagasaki, August 8, 1945, the Soviet Union declared war on Japan and the Red Army crossed the Manchurian frontier. There was in this event an unpleasant likeness to the Italian action in attacking France in 1940. Roosevelt's statement, "The hand that held the dagger has struck it into the back of its neighbor", could apply as well to the Soviet Union. However in this instance the United States was unfortunately an acces-

[2] Byrnes, *op. cit.*, pp. 208-09.
[3] *Ibid.*, pp. 208-09.

sory to what could, under different circumstances, be considered a crime.

For the USSR, the war lasted less than a week. Stalin therefore had no sooner announced the Soviet declaration of war on Japan than he was able to state that the Red Army had defeated Japan. In his victory message to the Soviet people on September 2, 1945, Stalin recalled that Japan had seized southern Sakhalin following the Soviet-Japanese War of 1904-05 and had invaded the Far Eastern Provinces following World War I. The Japanese, he remarked, caused repeated border incidents in Manchuria during 1938 and 1939. These events, plus the "defeat of Russian troops in 1904 in the period of the Russo-Japanese War," said Stalin, "left grave memories in the minds of our peoples. It was a dark stain on our country. Our people trusted and awaited the day when Japan would be routed and the stain wiped out. For forty years have we of the older generation waited for this generation, waited for this day. And now this day has come. Today Japan has acknowledged her defeat and signed the act of unconditional surrender. This means that southern Sakhalin and the Kurile Islands will pass to the Soviet Union, and from now on will not serve as a means for isolating the Soviet Union from the ocean and as a base for Japanese attacks on our Far East. They will serve, instead, as a means of direct communications of the Soviet Union with the ocean and as a base for the defense of our country against Japanese aggression."[4]

Needless to say, Stalin's assertions regarding the new Soviet acquisitions caused considerable concern among the general populations of the countries who had fought for so long against the Japanese. At that time the secret provisions of the Yalta Conference decisions were unpublished and Stalin's announcement consequently caused great speculation as to the extent of U.S.-British promises to Russia.

The day prior to Stalin's message, September 1, 1945, the Russian

[4] *New York Times,* September 3, 1945.
The following item appeared in the *New York Times,* September 5, 1945: "The Japanese Government began negotiations with the Soviet Union in June for 'conclusion of a treaty of amity and friendship and certain other matters'. The Japanese Government asserted that a reply to the overtures was being awaited when the Potsdam ultimatum was issued July 26, and implied that the Japanese surrender was delayed pending a reply from the Russians. On August 8, the Soviet announced that it had communicated to Naotake Sato, Japanese Ambassador in Moscow, that the Japanese proposal 'had lost its ground since Japan had repudiated the Potsdam Declaration and that the Soviet would enter into a state of war with Japan as from August 9.' " In this connection, Stalin related to Truman at Potsdam that the Japanese had approached the USSR and asked Stalin to act as mediator in a negotiated peace on various occasions, but that the Japanese had offered no specific proposals and consequently the Soviet had not given a reply.

Far Eastern Army completed the occupation of the 1,350 mile chain of Kurile Islands and of southern Sakhalin Island. The conquest placed Russia in control of the "Soviet Sea of Okhotsk" as Stalin called it,[5] the world's fourth largest sea. The Kuriles had once been the world's richest seal and sea otter hunting grounds and had figured prominently in Russo-Japanese relations during the nineteenth century. Russians had occupied the northernmost of these fog-bound islands until 1875, when Japan agreed to withdraw from Sakhalin in return for Russian withdrawal from the Kuriles. Russia had been later forced to give up southern Sakhalin by the Portsmouth Treaty of 1905. This territory had been sparsely populated by Russian sailors a century earlier, but proved unsuitable for purposes of large-scale colonization. Subsequent to the Portsmouth Treaty, however, both oil and coal were discovered on the northern part of the island and by an agreement of 1925 the Japanese had worked these deposits in conjunction with the Russians.

Historically, with the exception of the southern Kuriles, the Soviet Union had some basis for claiming the seized regions. Stalin had stressed that the recovery of Sakhalin and the Kuriles was a point of honor for the USSR and that their possession by Japan had been a "dark stain" on his country. However, there were other considerations in the Soviet desire for possession. Strategically, the Kuriles and all of Sakhalin form a ring of defense to the Pacific approaches of the Soviet Far East. Beyond this, they serve as waypoints for vessels beginning or completing the voyage across the Northern Sea Route from Vladivostok to Murmansk and Archangel.

Politically, the island of Kunashire, a few miles north of the Japanese main island of Hokkaido, comes as close as is possible to establishing a common border with Japan, and with it the resulting Communist influence that always accompanies proximity to the Soviet Union. Because of tight control by General MacArthur and the nature of Northern Hokkaido (cold and sparsely populated), however, Soviet influence deriving from proximity has so far been largely negligible in Japan.

As to economic possibilities, the USSR already controlled the areas of potential value in Northern Sakhalin. Ownership of the entire island merely provided for future unhampered exploitation by the Soviet Government. Sakhalin's material worth consists of limited deposits of coal and oil, as well as timber-lands, gold, and valuable adjoining fishing areas.

[5] *New York Times,* September 3, 1945.

For Communist doctrine as it applied to expansion, the gain was not important compared to European acquisitions. The Kuriles comprise approximately 4,000 square miles with a population density of slightly more than one person per mile. Southern Sakhalin, on the other hand, comprises 13,930 square miles and a population of 350,000. In that the population is largely Japanese it would be entirely feasible for the Supreme Soviet to construct a Japanese Autonomous Socialist Soviet Republic. This would be in direct line with the Soviet nationality policy and within both the spirit and letter of the Soviet Constitution. The ramifications of such an act are easy to imagine.

Thus with little more trouble than it takes to occupy new territory, Soviet Russia received generous compensation for less than one week of war with Japan. Her largest gains from the Yalta-promised war declaration, however, were on the Asian continent, where she expropriated, exploited, and plundered the territories of her ally, China. The scope of the Japanese aggrandizement was relatively small, but the scope of the Chinese aggrandizement that followed was of unimagined proportions, at least in the capitals of the west that unwittingly approved it.

CHAPTER 10

THE YALTA DECISIONS, CHINA, AND THE
SINO-SOVIET TREATY

". . . the Communist order or even the Soviet system cannot actually be introduced into China, because there do not exist the conditions for the successful establishment of either Communism or Sovietism."—Chinese Nationalist-USSR Joint Statement, 1923.

Six days after the atomic bomb destroyed Nagasaki and the Soviet Union declared war on Japan, and on the very day (August 14, 1945) that President Truman announced Japan's unconditional surrender, the USSR and China signed a Treaty of Alliance with supplementary agreements. Somewhat posthumously, Article I of this Sino-Soviet Treaty stated that the two powers agreed "to wage war against Japan until final victory."

According to the Yalta decisions, the Big Three had agreed that the USSR would receive far-reaching concessions from China providing that China herself could be brought to concur. This provision was assured when Roosevelt stated at Yalta that he would "take measures" to obtain the concurrence of Chiang Kai-shek. The Yalta decisions affecting China specified that the status quo in Outer Mongolia would be preserved; that the commercial port of Dairen would be internationalized with the pre-eminent interests of the Soviet Union recognized; that Port Arthur would be restored as a naval base to the USSR; and that the Chinese Eastern Railroad and the South Manchurian Railroad should be jointly operated by the establishment of a joint Soviet-Chinese company "it being understood that the pre-eminent interests of the Soviet Union be recognized." The Soviet Union was to receive all these concessions provided that it would declare war against Japan, and that it would conclude a pact of friendship and alliance with the Chinese "in order to render assistance to China with its armed forces for the purpose of liberating China from the Japanese yoke."

89

The Narkomindel evidently started negotiations with the Chinese Government shortly after the conclusion of the Crimea Conference in February 1945. Its demands, however, extended considerably beyond the terms agreed upon in the Yalta Agreement. Unconfirmed reports that the Soviet Union had bid for the huge Chinese island of Formosa appeared in the *New York Times* on May 11, 1945. This was supposedly in addition to Soviet proposals for Red Army occupation of Manchuria, and a protectorate over Korea.[1] By the time of Potsdam in July 1945, James F. Byrnes, then U.S. Secretary of State, had received a report that the USSR had brought increased pressure on the Chinese to accept excessive Russian territorial demands.[2] He immediately advised the Nationalist Government to resist Soviet pressure and to cede no rights other than those set forth by the Yalta Agreement. The Chinese evidently heeded Byrnes' advice and refused to yield to the Soviet demands. About this same time, Stalin and Molotov learned officially of the atomic bomb and took note of the Postdam Declaration. Faced with the immediate end of the war and the possibility that its Yalta promises would not be realized, the USSR lessened its demands and conceded some points to the usually unfortunate Chinese. On the very final moment of the war, therefore, the Soviet Union concluded an alliance and comprehensive agreements with China.

The Treaty of Alliance was not in itself of great significance, but the Supplementary Agreements restored the USSR to the pre-1905 position of Tsarist Russia and added significant embellishments as well. The first of these agreements provided that, after the Japanese armed forces had been expelled from Manchuria, two of the main railways, the Chinese Eastern and the South Manchurian, would be joined

[1] The status of Korea is unique but does not in itself yet fall in the category of territory directly aggrandized by the Soviet Union. The Koreans had been promised independence "in due course" by terms of the Cairo Declaration of 1943, but evidently no plans had been worked out between the Allied Powers as to how this should be brought about. Korea had been governed as part of Japan since 1910, and had little or no experience in self government. Apparently a last minute decision was reached between the U.S. and USSR whereby the former was to occupy territory south of the 38° and the latter, the northern sectors of the country. The purpose of this division was to facilitate the disarming of Japanese troops in Korea, but through a series of misunderstandings the areas continued under the military occupation of both nations. While several attempts have been made to clarify the situation, Korea is likely to remain a divided nation; her prospects for real independent statehood in the near future are dim. Korea and the USSR, incidentally, have a common border in the area of Changkufeng near the 43°.

[2] Byrnes, *op. cit.*, p. 205.

into one railway system called the Chinese Changchun Railway. "This railway system," said the agreement, "will become the joint property of the Soviet Union and the Chinese Republic and will be jointly exploited by them."

The end result of this agreement was that the Soviet Union in 1945 placed itself in almost the identical advantageous position held by Russia in 1904. The railway, which ran in a northerly direction from Dairen to Harbin in central Manchuria, and from there in a northwesterly direction to the Soviet Union, had the effect of cutting Manchuria in half. Moreover, the management and control of the railway was in the hands of the Soviet Government, and the contract and agreements gave certain aspects of sovereignty to the USSR.

The Second Supplementary Agreement concerned Port Arthur and added considerable weight to the railway agreement. It stated that "With the aim of strengthening the security of China and the USSR and the preventing of aggression again by Japan, the Government of the Chinese Republic agrees to joint utilization by both contracting parties of Port Arthur as a naval base." Furthermore, the agreement continued, the two parties "have agreed to turn Port Arthur into a purely naval base at the disposal of the battleships and merchant ships of China and the USSR alone." The administration of the base was put in the hands of three Soviet and two Chinese representatives. The Chairman was specifically required to be a Soviet citizen and the Vice Chairman a Chinese citizen. In addition to its control over administration, the Soviet Union was charged with defense of the naval base and was given the right to maintain its various armed forces and determine their location in the area. Along with the railroad agreement, this arrangement was to continue in force for thirty years.

The next concession by the Chinese concerned the port of Dairen. The preface to this agreement stated: "In view of the fact that the Treaty of Friendship and Alliance has been concluded between the USSR and the Chinese Republic, also of the fact that the USSR has guaranteed respect for Chinese sovereignty of the three Eastern Provinces (Manchuria) as an inseparable part of China, in order to insure the interests of the USSR in Dairen an import and export port of commodities, the Chinese Republic hereby expresses its consent:

"1. To proclaim Dairen a free port open to trade and shipping of all countries.

"2. To set aside for leasing to the USSR piers and warehouses in the said free port on the basis of separate agreements.

"3. Administration in Dairen will be exercised by China." But,

"The chief of the port shall be appointed from among Soviet citizens by the manager of the Changchun Railway by agreement with the Mayor of Dairen."

The Dairen arrangement was followed by an agreement concerning the relations between Soviet troops in Manchuria and Chinese Civil authorities. If one recalls that this agreement was signed the day that Japan accepted unconditional surrender and not ratified until more than a week later its wording assumes a unique character. It was titled (author's italics) "Agreement on relations . . . in conjunction with *the present joint war against Japan.*" According to the text, "(1) After the entry of Soviet troops as a *result of hostilities* into the three Eastern Provinces of China, supreme authority and responsibility in the zone of hostilities in all questions relating to the prosecution of the *war* for the period necessary for operations, shall rest with the commander in chief of the Soviet armed forces."

A subsequent clause provided extraterritorial jurisdiction for all persons under the command of Soviet armed forces in Manchuria. Thus, although it "confirmed its respect for China's full sovereignty over the three Eastern Provinces", the USSR became not only the "pre-eminent" power in Manchuria as assured by the U.S. and Britain at Yalta, but in fact exerted real control over this territory.

Shortly after the Red Army had overrun Manchuria, Molotov gave assurances that the victorious and liberating armed forces of the Soviet Union would begin evacuating the area three weeks after the capitulation of Japan and leave the territory completely within three months after the conclusion of hostilities.[3] However, the Red Army did not leave until the spring of 1946. And when it eventually did depart, Chinese Communist forces were able to seize control of the northern and eastern portions of the territory and render impossible both Nationalist Government control of this area and its participation in the Chinese Changchun Railway.[4] Actually, however, this railway had already established a Red ribbon of control across Manchuria from the Soviet Union to the extraterritorial concessions at Dairen and Port Arthur. The simple fact of the matter was that in all but name Manchuria had passed directly from Japanese to Communist control. The Nationalist Government of China, after more than ten years of des-

[3] *U.S. and World Affairs, op. cit.,* p. 295; *New York Times,* Aug. 27, 1945.

[4] In departing from this postwar occupation of Manchuria, the Soviet forces removed factories and equipment the worth of which in damage to China (including deterioration and replacement) was estimated at over two billion dollars, according to the Report of the Pauley Commission on industrial conditions in Manchuria. Department of State *Bulletin,* XV, December 22, 1946, pp. 1154-5.

perate war with Japan, was forced to place one of its richest territorial possessions under the control of the Soviet Union, which by the most generous estimates had been at war with Japan for only six days. Even when the Red Army departed, China was able to assert civil authority only in the southern portions of the territory, an authority that evaporated when Chinese Communist troops forced the few Chinese Nationalists out of Manchuria a short time later.

The methods used by the Soviet Union in Manchuria need little elucidation. The acquisition of the railway, Port Arthur, Dairen, and the resulting control of Manchuria, were guaranteed to the Soviet Government at Yalta by Roosevelt and Churchill. The Sino-Soviet Treaty merely formalized the Yalta Agreements. Soviet Russia exploited its control by the wholesale removal of Manchurian industry, 400 kilometers of railway trackage, and Manchurian transportation facilities; in addition, the USSR at least indirectly assisted Communist segments of the Chinse Army to gain control of the Manchurian areas eventually evacuated by the Red Army.

At the same time, the Soviets sought to secure economic control by demanding from the hapless Chinese joint ownership and administration of certain Japanese-developed heavy industry on the grounds that the USSR had defeated Japan in Manchuria and that this industry had been constructed for war use against the Soviet Union; in addition, the Soviets demanded commercial air rights and the construction of air fields throughout Manchuria and also the right to erect a Soviet-owned telephone line from Dairen to Manchouli on the Soviet border.[5]

The Chinese attempted at first to negotiate in regard to the Soviet demands, but eventually were compelled to abandon the negotiations, because such compelling proposals would have destroyed even the legend of Chinese sovereignty. Actually, the only valid purpose of the Kremlin in negotiating an agreement of this character was to legitimatize a *fait accompli.*

In the final analysis, although the professed reason for Soviet aggrandizement was that of revenge against the Japanese for the Russian defeat of 1905, the Russians took that revenge against the Chinese. The Soviet Union gained an ice-free naval base at Port Arthur and control of 29,000 Chinese; a commercial ice-free port at Dairen (which so far has been open only to the Soviet Union) and a population of 232,000; and a rail ribbon extending directly across Manchuria which assured the USSR a controlling position in this area. Although initially plundered in a momentary policy of opportunism, the economic and

---

[5] *New York Times,* January 17, 1946.

strategic worth of Manchuria can eventually prove as valuable to Communist Russia as it did to imperialist Japan.

Mongolia

Another important cession by the Chinese Government was the surrender of its final claim to Outer Mongolia. This area had actually long been controlled by the Soviet Union although nominally it still remained under the aegis of the Government of China. The Chinese reluctantly agreed in the Sino-Soviet Treaty of 1945 that "In view of the desire for independence repeatedly expressed by the people of Outer Mongolia, the Chinese Government declares that after Japan's defeat if a plebiscite of the people of Outer Mongolia confirm this desire, the Chinese Government will recognize the independence of Outer Mongolia in her existing boundaries."

This was the *coup de grace* to the last vestige of Chinese sovereignty. There were never any doubts that the results of the plebiscite would be favorable to a tacit Soviet protectorate over Outer Mongolia. But the USSR as usual desired to cloak its actions in the deceptive raiment of legality. The plebiscite was conducted between October 10 and October 20, 1945. According to official figures, it resulted in one of the most fantastic expressions of opinion or the collective mind the world has ever known. Out of the total population of approximately 840,000 some 483,291 of these semi-nomadic people voted and signed their names to the ballots. The final result showed 483,291 votes in favor of independence from China with no invalid ballots and not one voter in favor of continuing even outward allegiance to the Chinese.[6]

The Mongolians, of course, had been well trained. The vote showed that twenty-five years of Soviet indoctrination was not without effect. Ever since the 1921 treaty between the Mongols and the Russians, relations between the USSR and this country had become increasingly intimate. In spite of periodic declarations by Soviet officials that Chinese sovereignty was recognized and respected, the USSR pursued a policy of Soviet modernization of the territory by sending army instructors, employees of the government, specialists, doctors, and others to Mongolia. Furthermore, although supposedly recognizing Chinese sovereignty, the Soviet Government proceeded to conclude treaties with the so-called Mongolian People's Republic. In addition to the agreement of 1921, a Treaty of Friendship was signed in 1932, and a Mutual Assistance Pact was concluded March 12, 1936. Such acts by the Soviet Union in concluding treaties with an area of the Chinese Republic

6 *New York Times,* October 24, 1945.

would be somewhat analogous to pre-war Japan concluding similar treaties with the pre-war U. S. Commonwealth of the Philippines. This consideration, however, did not appear to concern the Soviet Union in its dealings with a weak and disorganized China. On the contrary, there is every indication that the very opposite was the case.

Even before Mongolia achieved an alleged independence, the People's Government took it upon itself to declare war on Japan in collaboration with the Soviet Union (although technically, as Chinese territory, Mongolia had been at war with Japan for many years). A Tass dispatch of August 11, 1945, reported that the Monoglian People's Government, had declared a "Holy War" on Japan. The Mongolian declaration said in part: "prompted by a fraternal attitude towards the peoples of the Soviet Union who have extended to us—the Mongolian people—their fraternal, helping hand in the reestablishment and strengthening of our state independence, true to obligations under the Treaty of Mutual Assistance March 12, 1936, hereby declare a holy war against Japan on the side of the United Nations."

Although published only three days before the end of the Japanese War, this declaration was among the first postwar moves by the Soviet Union to increase its voice in world affairs, particularly in the United Nations. It indicated a significant change in Soviet concepts of aggrandizement. The new policy of the USSR sought when possible to maintain the legal existence of the actually aggrandized state. This method was designed to give increased Soviet representation in international affairs, a supposedly wide popular basis supporting world communism, and the apparent impression that the Soviet Union was no longer pursuing a policy of territorial aggrandizement. Historical evidence indicates that had the independence of Outer Mongolia been recognized by China previous to World War II, a Mongolian plebiscite would have expressed the desire of the people for Mongolia to become a Soviet Republic, and in turn the Supreme Soviet would have granted this request almost automatically. The Kremlin postwar policy was to create ostensibly independent states, however—a major shift pre-indicated by the Soviet constitutional change of February 1, 1944, giving Soviet Republics the right to conclude treaties and carry on diplomatic relations with foreign states.[7] It is also evident in the Soviet-created "People's Democracies" of Eastern Europe.

The immediate objective of the USSR in the case of Outer Mongolia, was to increase Russia's voice in Asiatic affairs. More specifically,

---

[7] Supreme authority, of course, still remained with the Communist Party of the Soviet Union, an extra-constitutional but nonetheless final authority.

the intention was to provide the Soviets with an additional vote on the Far Eastern Commission, and to magnify the USSR claim for Japanese reparations. Accordingly, Marshal Choibalsan, the head of the Mongolian People's Republic, stated that his country was "one of the bulwarks of peace in the Far East" and had been an "effective barrier against extension of the aggressive designs of Japanese imperialists" since 1921. Furthermore, his country had suffered 675 casulties in aiding the Russian conquest of Manchuria.[8] This casualty record was remarkable in view of the fact that the Mongolians had entered the war three days before the unconditional surrender of Japan and many hours after all fighting had ceased on the Far Eastern front. The Kremlin also had in mind an additional vote for itself in the United Nations General Assembly, if it were possible to convince that body that Outer Mongolia was a sovereign state. However, the fiction of sovereignty maintained by Outer Mongolia did not prove acceptable to the independent states of the United Nations.

The good feeling and mutual trust between the Mongols and the USSR resulted in a Mutual Assistance Pact, signed February 27, 1946, which provided for military and other aid in the event of an armed attack by a third party. But there were indications that the terms of the pact went much further than the published text. On July 18, 1946, the *New York Times* reported that the "Chinese Foreign Office had learned of a secret deal between the Soviet Union and the Mongolian People's Republic permitting the garrisoning of Russian troops in that pivotal Asian state. The Nanking Government is reacting sensitively," said the *Times*, "to a projected Soviet garrison in Mongolia which is the strategic key to China's backdoor."

China evidently had good reason for concern. Reports appeared periodically that Soviet influence was becoming increasingly strong throughout Inner Mongolia as well. There was information to the effect that Communist-sponsored autonomous regimes had been formed on at least two different occasions.[9] That these reports later ceased to appear was probably due to the subsequent control of this area by Chinese Communist troops. However, there remained the possibility that the Soviets would exploit the idea of Pan-Mongolism from both the Mongolian People's Republic and the Buryat-Mongol Autonomous Soviet Republic, if and when the occasion called for such action. The Russians have profitably used the method whereby a national group within the USSR has proclaimed itself the true representative of all

8 *New York Times,* October 26, 1946.
9 *Ibid.,* October 23, 1945; February 12, 1946.

peoples of that nationality regardless of in what country these people might be situated. This has been particularly true of the various nationalities situated on either side of the Soviet Eurasian border. The USSR has concocted still another noteworthy method of aggrandizement for the peoples of the Asiatic borderlands. On the basis of its nationality policy, the USSR has laid great stress on the development of backward, nomadic peoples, particularly those on either side of the Soviet border. This development has taken the form of educational programs, cultural, industrial, and agricultural projects, and the construction of modern cities near the frontier, thus attracting the backward peoples living on the opposite side of the Soviet border toward the benefits gained and progress made by their own nationality within the USSR. There is no denying that the Soviet nationality policy has been a source of great strength in the Communist program of aggrandizement.

In the case of Outer Mongolia, the Soviet Union provided material and cultural development for a nomadic race which had remained virtually stagnate since the days of Ghengis Khan. The improvement of their situation was noticed, of course, by Mongols living in Inner Mongolia, many of whom naturally desired to better their own lot in life. It is obvious that this method will work good effect as long as the Soviet Union encounters peoples materially more backward and undeveloped than its own. And there are tens of millions of them in Asia. When, on the other hand, the reverse is true the Soviet Union has to rely on different methods or else suffer the consequences of its own tactics.

As to the economics of expansion into Mongolia, there have been tangible benefits. The Russians constructed a railway running from the Trans-Siberian line to Ulan Bator, the Mongolian capital. From there, a well-developed motorable trade route ran across Outer Mongolia to North China. There is in addition considerable pasture land in the country for sheep and cattle which have supplied great quantities of hides to the Soviet economy. Moreover, there remain supposedly unexploited areas of considerable mineral wealth in Mongolia.

In regard to strategy, the Mongolian People's Republic serves as a buffer for Soviet Siberia. It is an excellent zone of defense for the Trans-Siberian railway in the event that any hostile power attempts to operate in that direction from North China.

Tannu-Tuva

When China accepted the result of the Mongolian plebiscite and surrendered her claim to Outer Mongolia, she also surrendered any claim she might have had to Urianghia or Tannu-Tuva. This region is probably as little known to foreigners as any other area in Asia. Located at the northwest corner of Outer Mongolia, the area of Tannu-Tuva is about one-third that of Spain and the population is approximately 70,000. The people are Urian-Khai Mongols, akin to the neighboring Soviet Buryats. The country itself is extremely mountainous and takes in the basin at the source of the Yenisei River. The valley of this river, which, incidentally, runs towards the Arctic, and air transport are practically the only methods of entrance into the country. Tannu-Tuva is supposedly extremely rich both in agricultural and mineral resources and has the potentialities for large scale hydro-electric power development. Its strategic worth lies in its central position between Mongolia, Chinese Turkestan, and Soviet Asia. Control of this territory by the USSR makes the southern approaches to Siberia nearly impregnable.[10]

Neither China nor Russia until recent times has ever maintained a very effective claim to the territory. Prior to 1911, Tannu-Tuva was considered an area of Outer Mongolia, but with the disintegration of the Chinese Empire it supposedly became a Russian protectorate in 1914. On August 13, 1921, the Tannu-Tuvians declared their independence, drew up a constitution and established the Tannu-Tuva Republic. Apparently this desire for independence received the support of the Soviet Government. A Russian delegation attended the original constituent assembly. Less than a month later, on September 9, 1921, the Soviet Government repudiated the former Tsarist rights of protector, recognized Tannu-Tuva's independence, and established diplomatic relations with that country.[11] The Mongolian People's Republic did likewise. From that time until 1945, little was known of this nation except that a few postage stamps were issued and in great demand by stamp collectors.

Then, in April 1945, Tannu-Tuva was omitted from the Soviet diplomatic list as a foreign country. On October 1, 1945, the list of Soviet Russian electoral districts included the "Tuvian Autonomous Oblast."[12] From all indications this Oblast or District was the former sovereign state of Tannu-Tuva which evidently had been incorporated

[10] Fedor S. Mansvetov, "Russia and China in Outer Mongolia," *Foreign Affairs*, October 1945; Davidson-Houston, "Russia in Asia," *Royal Central Asian Journal*, July-October 1946.

[11] For additional material on this subject, see Fedor S. Mansvetov, *Ibid*. Also Owen Lattimore, "The Outer Mongolian Horizon," *Ibid.*, July 1946, pp. 648-61. Also Lt. Col. Davidson-Houston MBE, "Russia in Asia," *op. cit.*

[12] *New York Times*, February 18, 1947.

without plebiscite or treaty. In actual practice, after its declaration of independence in 1921, Tannu-Tuva doubtless continued as a Soviet Russian protectorate, but the complete absence of that formal legality which almost without exception characterizes Soviet actions was a striking contrast in the absorption of this state.

It is difficult to arrive at any valid conclusions as to the original Soviet purpose in creating Tannu-Tuva as an independent state in 1921 when the tendency at that time was to incorporate new territories into the USSR as Soviet Socialist Republics. On the other hand, it is equally difficult to conclude why, when the tendency was to establish Communist governments within existing legal governmental structures, the Soviet Union suddenly abolished Tannu-Tuva and incorporated the area into the Russian Soviet Republic. A pure supposition would be that in the first case, the Soviet Government, weak and facing extinction from outside sources, established an independent government in impregnable Tannu-Tuva, where a Communist regime could continue to exist regardless of the fate of Russia and the Soviet Union. In the latter case when Tannu-Tuva was abolished, a more rigid control of the area might have been desired by the Soviets for purposes of security. It will be recalled that Tannu-Tuva contains extensive mineral resources, great potential hydro-electric power, and is in one of the most isolated, inaccessible regions in Asia.

Sinkiang

Another Supplementary Agreement to the Sino-Soviet Treaty stated, "As to the latest events in Sinkiang the Soviet Government confirms that it has no intention to interfere with China's internal affairs." "The latest events in Sinkiang" as of 1945 were large-scale revolts by the native population and fighting with Chinese Nationalist troops. Evidently a considerable portion of the population, ninety-four percent of whom were not Chinese, had tired of Chinese minority misrule. In 1944 revolts had begun in Sinkiang which by 1945 were so serious that the Nationalist Government had been forced to dispatch large detachments of troops to the area. The troops, however, had not been entirely successful in quelling the uprisings.

The ostensible reason for the rebellion was the oppressive colonial policy pursued by the Nationalists. Only six percent of the population were Chinese, while more than seventy-five percent were Turki, ten percent Kazakh, and the remainder Tungans, Kirghiz, Mongols, White Russians, Tartars, Uzbeks, and Tajiks.

Although Sinkiang was divided by economic, political, and religious cleavages which cut directly across the nationality pattern, the main issues were racial and national in character.

Historically, China proclaimed Sinkiang, or Chinese Turkestan, a province in 1882. Following the collapse of the Manchus in 1911, it came under warlord rule. The most recent of these warlords had been General Sheng Shih-tsai who had reigned from 1934 until 1943. Sheng had called in the Russians to help them rule, and for eight years Soviet influence had been supreme in the province. Large sums of money were spent by the USSR on barracks, factories, and airfields. Sheng's regime, however, was one of gross misrule. Thousands of the population were imprisoned and thousands were liquidated. In 1942, Sheng presumably became convinced that the USSR would lose the war or else felt that his power was insecure. Consequently, he violently extirpated all traces of Soviet influence. At that time, the USSR was occupied with crucial battles in the west and so was compelled to accept this situation. Sheng's misrule, however, had been also of concern to the Chinese Nationalist Government, and early in 1943 he was eased out of control by Chiang Kai-shek. His replacement was General Wu Chung-hsin, the first governor ever appointed by the Nationalist Government. Unfortunately, however, the damage done by Sheng was beyond repair.[13]

On November 7, 1944, the three northern districts of Sinkiang—Ili, Chuguchak, and Altai, all of which bordered on the Soviet Union—revolted and proclaimed a Republic of East Turkestan. This was a severe blow to China in that these three are the most prosperous of the ten districts in Sinkiang. They produce not only a surplus of grain but also oil, wolfram, and gold. The population consists of approximately 53% Kazakh and 23% Turki. There were some indications that these Kazakhs and the "East Turkestan Republic" received considerable aid from the bordering Kazakh Soviet Republic.[14]

Presumably to bring peace to Sinkiang the Soviet Consul in Urumchi, capital of the province, offered to act as mediator in order to bring about a settlement between the Ili districts and the Chinese. The offer was accepted and a peace agreement was negotiated which gave the three districts a degree of autonomy and self-rule, but at the same time recognized Chinese authority. However, the solution did not last. By the autumn of 1947, the leaders of the Ili districts had denounced the agreement and reasserted their independence. Nationalist troops were unsuccessful in an attempt to reestablish Chinese control.[15]

13 *Times*, London, September 22-23, 1948 and *New York Times*, February 1, 1948.
14 *Times*, London, September 22-23, 1948.
15 *Ibid.*

Propaganda issuing from the revolted areas was reported to possess a striking similarity to that of the People's Republics in Eastern Europe. Charges were made that the Chinese Government was "obstructing the organization of democratic bodies, organizing reactionary bodies" and "oppressing progressive elements."[16]

By the fall of 1948, the cleavage between the Nationalist Government and the Ili groups was beyond remedy. Both the Nationalists and the rebels aimed at complete control of Sinkiang, and apparently would accept nothing less.

In an analysis of the Sinkiang situation, it was apparent from all reports that the Soviet Union did not live up to the terms of the Sino-Soviet Agreement. On the contrary, it seems certain that the USSR desired a pre-eminent role in Sinkiang as well as in Manchuria and Mongolia. Competent sources reported that although the Soviets probably had no part in the original Turki and Kazakh revolt, it was exploited to Soviet ends at an early stage. There was strong evidence, moreover, that the USSR supplied most of the arms and ammunition for the rebels, and in addition supplied the Ili group with military, economic, and political advisers. Furthermore, Young Communists were said to have infiltrated into the region from the neighboring Kazakh Soviet Republic.[17]

The motives of the USSR in detaching the three northern Ili districts from Sinkiang were in part strategic. Sinkiang is within striking distance of the Turksib Railway, and the Soviets were obviously anxious to insure that this Chinese province maintained a friendly regime. Moreover, through Sinkiang passes an ancient highway between Central Asia and the Far East. Under Soviet control the prospects of penetrating East Asia are quite apparent.

The matter of strategic security, however, was decidedly not of primary importance. China was certainly in no position to threaten either the Turksib Railway or the Soviet territories to the north. Japan was a defeated, disarmed nation. And any other power which could be considered a possible threat to the USSR was thousands of miles away from Sinkiang.

The primary objects of Soviet policy in Sinkiang were the potential economic wealth, the land mass itself, and the population which is also indigenous to the bordering Soviet Republics. The Soviet Union was materially aided in its attempts to win over Sinkiang by economic

16 *Times*, London, September 22-23, 1948; *New York Times*, February 1, 1948.

17 For additional material on Sinkiang: *Times*, London, *op. cit.*; *New York Times*, January 26, 1945; May 16, 17, 18, 1945; June 3, 1946; February 1, 1948. Also Davidson-Houston, *op. cit.*

geographical factors. For instance, the economic orientation of the natural trade routes is towards Russian Siberia. For the Sinkiang merchants it is much easier to market goods through the relatively well-developed roads and the Turksib Railway of the USSR than to transport materials 2,000 miles to the Yangtze. Moreover, since these routes to the USSR ran through the rebel Ili districts, the Soviets exerted an added measure of economic control on the rest of Sinkiang.

Chinese maladministration also played into Soviet hands. Notoriously corrupt, inefficient, and harsh, the Chinese administrators have traditionally done much to alienate the Sinkiang population. Furthermore, until 1946, Chinese had been the only official language in the territory although the vast majority of the population spoke Turki. All in all, the Chinese administration had committed a series of tragic mistakes. The USSR on one hand exploited the resentment of the native population at Chinese misrule and on the other pointed with pride to the professed accomplishments of the kindred Kazakhs, Kirghiz, Turkis, and Tajiks in the neighboring Soviet Republics. At the same time, the Soviets kindled the nationalist aspirations of the Turki majority. Propaganda about schools, hospitals, hydro-electric plants, scientific production, etc., proved quite successful with a population that had few or none of these material advantages. In spite of the natural antagonism of the predominantly Moslem population toward Communism, a considerable number doubtless felt that they had little to lose and perhaps something to gain by association with the Soviet Republics to the north.

The gains in natural resources for the USSR included increased supplies of wool, tea, tung oil, tungsten and other minerals. From a political standpoint, control of the three northern districts of Sinkiang permitted the USSR to exert a strong influence on the seven remaining districts, whose mastery provides a formidable geographic border with Tibet as well as an equally difficult border with India and Afghanistan. Furthermore, while the Soviet Union was enticing the Turkis and Kazakhs of Sinkiang to the glories of the USSR, it was simultaneously satisfying the nationalist aspirations of these same peoples within the Soviet Union. In all probability, many Kazakh and Turki citizens of the USSR were firmly convinced that it was their sacred duty to liberate their unfortunate brothers from Chinese oppression.

Territorially, the wartime gains of the Soviet Union in the Far East were tremendous. They were achieved primarily through encroachments on Soviet Russia's hapless ally, China, and they were realized with the assistance of the United States and Great Britain. What is more important, these additions were in turn responsible for even greater Communist gains at the expense of the Chinese, gains which were to place a large part of East Asia under at least the indirect control of the Kremlin. From the appearances of Soviet aggrandizement in China, the search for security would not end until all the world were secure.

CHAPTER 11

SCANDINAVIA AND CZECHOSLOVAKIA

His Tongue
Dropt Manna, and could make the worse appear
The better reason, to perplex and dash
Maturest Counsels.

—*Milton, "Paradise Lost."*

No country and no people along the thousands of miles of Soviet border from the North Pacific through Asia and Europe to the North Atlantic has escaped the territorial acquisitiveness of the USSR. Norway, which acquired a common border with Soviet Russia for the first time after World War II, was no exception.[1]

The new Russo-Norwegian border became a recognized fact when the Soviet Union acquired the Petsamo district from Finland at the end of World War II and, strangely, Russia and Norway had little trouble delineating this new frontier. The USSR advanced no historic claims, had no kindred feeling for the inhabitants of northern Norway, evidently felt that the region was of little economic value, decided that the Finnmark border area had a limited strategic importance and in Norwegian possession did not endanger the security of the Soviet Union. Therefore, from August 2-16, 1946, the delegates of the two nations sat in comparative harmony in Moscow and plotted out the new border. Utilizing documents and maps defining the 1826 border with certain additional amendments made in 1896, the commission made no changes in the nineteenth-century boundary. The only decision of importance was that the border should be clearly marked in order to avoid any trespassing disputes. These, incidentally, had been frequent from the time the Red Army evacuated the Finnmark area following World War II.

[1] Tsarist Russia had a common border with Norway until the independence of Finland following World War I.

Of far greater importance were Soviet demands for Norwegian territory in the Arctic. In November 1944 the Kremlin summoned the Norwegian Foreign Minister, then Trygve Lie, for what apparently were routine discussions on relations between the two countries. After only a short stay in Moscow, Lie returned to Oslo. All indications at the time suggested that Norwegian-Soviet affairs would continue to be normal and that nothing unusual had transpired during the discussions. Similar meetings took place at least once in 1945, but were outwardly of no great importance. Then rumors began to appear in the autumn of 1945 that the Soviet Government was making demands for Spitsbergen Island to the north of Norway.[2] They were not confirmed, however, until January 9, 1946.

The USSR, it seemed, had originally asked Norway for both military bases on the Norwegian island of Spitsbergen and outright possession of nearby Bear Island. Norway, despite the overwhelming power her neighbor could bring to bear, rejected the Russian demands, but nevertheless felt it advisable to continue discussions. The USSR then suggested a joint regional defense system for that part of the Arctic, designed to operate within the framework of the United Nations. This Soviet plan included joint defense of the Spitsbergen archipelago by Norway and the Soviet Union. The Norwegians, however, succeeded in putting off a direct answer until the USSR mentioned the subject again late in 1946. Apparently convinced that the matter could be delayed no longer, Norway discreetly allowed the secret Soviet demands to be made public.

The news caused both annoyance and concern among Russia's wartime allies. For the Kremlin's edification it was immediately pointed out by the West that Norway's "full and absolute" sovereignty over Spitsbergen had been guaranteed by a treaty signed in Paris in 1920.[3] The sovereignty award was on the condition that Norway would agree neither to create nor to allow the establishment of any naval base nor to construct any fortifications on the archipelago, and furthermore that the islands would "never be used for warlike purposes." The original signatories, in addition to Norway, were the United States, United

[2] Pertinax, *New York Times*, October 17, 1945; November 19, 1945.

[3] Prior to 1920, no country held legal possession of Spitsbergen. Conflicting claims were advanced at one time or another by the British, Dutch, Swedes, Danes, Russians, and Americans. Conferences to settle the issue in 1910, 1912, and 1914 were unsuccessful. In 1919, the Allied Supreme Council granted Norway sovereignty over the Spitsbergen archipelago. This act was validated by a treaty (mentioned above) signed in Paris, February 9, 1920.

Kingdom, France, Japan, Italy, Sweden, and the Netherlands. In addition, twenty-three other governments, including the Soviet Union in 1935, had subsequently adhered to the treaty.[4]

Once the news of the negotiations had become known, Moscow sought to justify its unusual action on four primary contentions. First, the treaty of 1920 was invalid because among the signatories were states that had fought against the Allied Powers in World War II. Second, the 1920 treaty was signed "without the knowledge of the Soviet Union and without its participation" (disregarding the fact that the USSR had formally adhered to the treaty in 1935). Third, because existing conditions had completely changed from those of 1920, the treaty was not in accordance with the present status of the Soviet Union. And fourth, "the treaty completely disregarded the security and economic interests" of the USSR.[5]

Regardless of these justifications, Soviet Russia had in fact attempted to violate her treaty obligations and ignore completely her obligations to other signatory nations. In February 1947, however, the Kremlin's maneuvers were completely frustrated when the Norwegian Storting or Parliament decided against entering into bilateral discussions regarding Spitsbergen military questions.[6] The Norwegians politely suggested that if the Soviet Government desired to alter the existing status of the Spitsbergen archipelago, it was a question for discussion among the signatory powers of the 1920 treaty and for the United Nations.

Undoubtedly, the primary basis for this Soviet territorial demand was security and strategic advantage. A Tass dispatch of January 14, 1947, revealed that in regard to "the problem of USSR security, as it has been clearly proved by the Second World War, the Spitsbergen islands lying at the western outlet to the ocean are of exceptional importance in this respect for the USSR in the north." Needless to say, the particular interest of the USSR in Spitsbergen, at a time when the Allied Powers were entering the final months of the European War, was an indication to some that Soviet Russia's long-range Arctic strategy was concerned with security against attack across the polar regions. Conversely, Soviet strategists were doubtless aware that Spitsbergen was an offensive necessity as well. The industrial regions of North America are only 3,500 air-miles from Spitsbergen.

4 *New York Times,* January 11, 1947.

5 *New Times,* Moscow, February 7, 1947. Also for other events relating to this subject: *New York Times,* January 10, 11, 15, 1947. Tass dispatches, January 14, 15, 1947.

6 *New York Times,* March 4, 1947.

As for economic considerations, the USSR already operated under lease a few coal mines on Spitsbergen. Norwegians have estimated that there are potentially eight billion tons of coal in the nearly 24,000 square miles of archipelago. Mining, however, has yet to be conducted on a very great scale. Prior to the war, approximately 700,000 tons of coal were mined annually of which the Russians claimed they mined 400,000 tons. Of the forty mines on the islands, however, the Russians owned only four, the Norwegians thirty-two, and a Scottish concern four.[7] The Soviets used the coal extractions for the operation of their Arctic fleet, and the Norwegians used the coal for domestic purposes in northern Norway. But although the coal reserves were an important consideration, they were in fact of little more importance to the USSR than some 3,000 miners who inhabited the islands. The Soviet desire for acquisition was based primarily upon strategic concepts. The unique methods it had used toward this end were as unfruitful as the ostensible reasons it had advanced for control of the island.

But in spite of the Norwegian rebuff the Soviet Government continued to maintain a strong interest in the land areas of the far north. There were periodic reports that Norwegian sealers had found it increasingly difficult to work the waters in the vicinity of Franz Josef Land, the Russian islands directly to the east of Spitsbergen.[8] Although of less value strategically, these islands flank the Norwegian islands, and, in the event of any conflict, make it improbable that Spitsbergen can be used by any power against the Soviet Union.

Denmark

The Soviet Union has had no common border with Denmark. The Danes, however, possess Bornholm Island in the lower part of the Baltic Sea, an island occupied by a German garrison during World War II. Bornholm itself is of no particular significance as long as it is under the sovereignty of a small power such as Denmark. But in the hands of a great power it is strategically in a position to control the entrance to the Baltic Sea.

On May 8, 1945, a few days after the German forces capitulated in Europe, General Eisenhower decided to send an Allied landing force to occupy Bornholm and disarm the German garrison there, but before doing so he asked the Soviet High Command if such an operation would interfere with Red Army plans. The Soviet officers replied that, "in view of the fact the Germans [on Bornholm] were within the sphere

[7] *New York Times,* April 15, 1947.
[8] *Ibid.*

of operation of Soviet armed forces and that the commander of the German garrison had requested assistance with food, the island was being occupied by Soviet forces."[9]

Consequently, at 2:45 p.m. on May 9, 1945, Russian forces landed on the island. The German garrison surrendered immediately. The Red Air Force nevertheless bombed Bornholm and caused considerable destruction to the small villages and farms of the island.[10] Less than a week later, on May 15, 1945, the newly arrived Red Army garrison of roughly 2,500 men cut the telephone lines to the Danish mainland. This action was naturally a cause of high concern to the Danish Government, but its only recourse was to protest ineffectively. Nevertheless Danish hopes for a quick evacuation of the Red Army were heightened shortly thereafter when the USSR announced that the last German soldier had been removed from the island. But this optimism was short-lived, for the Red Army made no move to evacuate. On the contrary, it appeared that the Soviets were making plans to stay on for an indefinite period.[11]

Kai Myring, a *New York Times* correspondent, visited the island in the latter part of May 1945, a few days after the Soviet occupation commenced. Although he spent the first few hours of his stay being questioned by Red Army officials, Myring managed to spend three days on Bornholm before returning by boat to Sweden. He reported that Soviet influence was predominant and that the Red Army, from all appearances, was making preparations for a protracted stay. The Soviet soldiers, he said, were already referring to the island as "Russian Denmark."[12]

Some seven months after the Red Army first moved onto the island and an equal period after VE Day, in December 1945, it was reported that the Red Army had increased its Bornholm garrison to 6,000 men.[13] Some circles interpreted the Soviet stay as a counter-action to U. S. negotiations for air and weather stations on Iceland. Whatever the case, a little more than three months later, on March 17, 1946, the Red Army suddenly began to evacuate Bornholm.

The basis of the Soviet action was somewhat complex. Strategically, of course, Bornholm was of considerable value to the USSR and in this respect there were indications that the Soviet occupation was a carefully premeditated action. Russian occupation had been fore-

9 *New York Times*, March 4, 1947.

10 *Ibid.*, May 10, 27, 1945.

11 *Ibid.*, May 15, 16, 1945.

12 *Ibid.*, May 27, 1945.

13 *Ibid.*, Dec. 7, 1945.

shadowed as early as April 1945 when the Moscow radio announced that the Red Army intended to occupy points in Denmark. A possible explanation of this move and others like it appeared in a *Pravda* dispatch transmitted to Paris on May 27, 1945. "The Soviet Union," it proclaimed, "is a great democratic power capable of assuring the security not only of its own frontiers but also of the peoples of Europe, and the sooner this is recognized the better it will be for humanity."[14] Almost a year later, the Moscow *New Times* of April 1, 1946, stated that the Soviet withdrawal had caught the reactionary slanderers unawares, especially those who had accused the Soviet Union of converting Bornholm into a "Russian Malta in the Baltic". The Danes, the article said, were eternally grateful to "their liberators" who had "crushed the German hordes which continued to offer resistance."

The hard fact of the matter, however, was that the Russian position had become politically untenable. The Danish Communist Party asked the USSR to evacuate Bornholm lest the Party suffer in the general election of 1946.[15] Since the Danish elections were free, by Western definition, there was every reason to believe that the local Communists would have suffered severely had the Russians stayed on. Moreover, the probable pressure of the United Nations and the increased hostility of Scandinavia and Western Europe were among the disturbing consequences of continued Soviet occupation. Rather than face these complications in addition to those then arising from her aggressive actions in Iran and Turkey, Soviet Russia withdrew her forces from the Danish Island of Bornholm.

The withdrawal was of course heralded by the Moscow press as a typical example of Soviet good faith. It is more likely, however, that the Politburo sought to bring a measure of temporary relief to the Western World. Soviet experience indicated that a noisy withdrawal or concession in one sector usually resulted in a relaxation of the defensive Western attitude and made possible a quick intensified drive against another target. Since the Soviet border is the longest in the world it is easy to swing back and forth on the Eurasian axis continually applying pressure at widely separate points. In the case of Bornholm it was very feasible to make a strategic withdrawal with few if any losses and at the same time to apply pressure at another sector of the long frontier—at Turkey and Iran for instance. Russia was willing, in other words, to take one step backwards if she could take two steps forward.

[14] *New York Times,* May 29, 1945.
[15] *Ibid.,* January 19, 1947.

Czechoslovakia

The Soviet Union was more successful with its scheme of aggrandizement in Czechoslovakia than it was in Scandinavia. Early in 1943, Moscow raised the question of Ruthenia (known also as the Carpatho-Ukraine, and the Transcarpathian Ukraine) with the Czechoslovak Government in London. This region, said Moscow, contained a population predominantly Ukrainian, and it was therefore only right that it should be reunited with its Ukrainian homeland. Such reasoning overlooked the fact that Ruthenia had been a part of Czechoslovakia for the previous twenty-five years and before that a part of the Kingdom of Hungary for 800 years.[16] Nevertheless, this backward region of some 4,921 square miles and 725,000 people contained a population akin to the Ukrainians. Sixty-five percent of the inhabitants were "brother Ruthenians", and the remainder of the population comprised some fifteen percent Jews, fifteen percent Hungarians, and five percent Czechoslovaks. These minority groups, in turn, were subjects for the use of the expansionist Soviet multinational policy when and if a future occasion demanded it.

Soviet insistence that the Czechs cede Ruthenia was reiterated early in January 1945. At that time the Red Army had just liberated parts of Czechoslovakia from the Germans and the Kremlin felt that the territorial matter had to be settled at once. Ivan Petrushka, a Ruthenian Communist and at one time a member of the Czech Cabinet, presented the Czech President, Dr. Benes, with a demand that the area in question be transferred to the Ukrainian Soviet Republic. A plebiscite had been held, he claimed, resulting in an overwhelming mandate for Ruthenia to become a part of the Ukraine.[17]

Moscow, meanwhile, maintained that it was taking a non-committal attitude in the matter. The affair was one of purely Ukrainian interest, implied the Soviets, and would be handled by the Foreign Ministry of the Ukrainian Soviet Republic at Kiev. Nevertheless, Dr. Benes sought further clarification on the issue. He reminded the Russians that demands for Czechoslovak territory were not in accord with previous statements by Soviet leaders. Moscow artfully replied that the campaign for incorporation of Ruthenia was inspired by local Ukrainian authorities and would be officially discouraged.[18]

[16] Ruthenia, after considerable discussion amongst its leaders, decided to vote for union with Czechoslovakia in 1918, and was officially affixed to the state in 1919. It was incorporated as an autonomous territory with special guarantees being given for the preservation of its cultural autonomy.

[17] *New York Times*, January 20, 1945; *Economist* (London) January 20, 1945.

[18] *New York Times*, January 31, 1945.

By April, Sdeneck Fierlinger, Premier of Czechoslovakia, apparently had received more specific ideas on the subject from Moscow. "The question of the Carpatho-Ukraine," he reported, will be settled in accordance "with the wishes of the Ukrainian population of that region."[19] This statement inferred that the Czech Government would cede the region to the USSR. The kindred Ruthenians, it will be recalled, had allegedly conducted a plebiscite among themselves and expressed their desire to become a part of the Ukraine. Therefore, the matter was apparently settled. Thus with no more formality than the alleged plebiscite, on June 29, 1945, the Czech Government continued its disastrous policy of seeking to appease both East and West and ceded Ruthenia to the Soviet Union.

The cession, according to the Soviets, reunited Ruthenia "with her ancient motherland" and it was now rightfully a part of the Ukrainian Soviet Republic. The action was taken, the treaty of cession stated, "in accordance with desire shown by the population of the Carpatho-Ukraine and on a basis of friendly agreement of both high contracting parties."

Although the loss of the area to their Soviet ally was doubtless irritating to many Czechs, Ruthenia was not in itself a great material sacrifice. The region had been attached to Czechoslovakia by the Treaty of St. Germain-en-Laye, September 10, 1919. A wooded, mountainous region, Ruthenia has been noted primarily for a limited lumber production and a few small cellulose and match factories. Moreover, the Czechs themselves had poured considerable money into the area with little return on the investment. Economically, it was of slight value to the Prague Government.

To the Soviet Union, on the other hand, the region was of great value. Geographically it extended the USSR across a traditional boundary of Europe, the Carpathian Mountains. In line with Soviet Russia's policy of seeking common frontiers, the acquisition established a new border with Hungary, and consequently not only a firmer influence on Hungary but also a still stronger voice in the direction of Central European affairs.

Communist theoreticians naturally found it difficult to claim that the 725,000 people of Ruthenia had been liberated from the capitalist tyranny of the brother Czechs. However, it was expeditiously recalled by Moscow scholars that Ruthenia had been under foreign domination for nearly one thousand years and that "the oppression of the Hungarian feudal lords left its mark on the hole subsequent history of the

[19] *New York Times,* April 11, 1945.

Transcarpathian Ukrainians who remained one of the most backward people in Europe both economically and culturally."[20]

Be that as it may, the most revealing particular in the aggrandizement of Ruthenia was the operation of the Soviet policy of multinationalism. In this case, it was the same powerful Ukrainian nationalism that had already extended the Soviet Union into Bessarabia, Bucovina, Galicia, and Poland.

But the Ukrainian phase of multinational expansionism had apparently been completed with the absorption of Ruthenia. On November 6, 1945, Molotov proclaimed that the Soviet Ukraine now embraced territories in a fraternal union of which the Ukrainian brothers had dreamed for centuries.[21] The satisfaction of Ukrainian nationalism and the desire for a common border with Hungary had thus been one of the primary concepts of Soviet aggrandizement. The strategic motivation was one of secondary importance in that the region had previously been a part of a subservient Czechoslovakia. The only inherent contradiction in the otherwise neat operation was that Ukrainian nationalism and expansion had clashed with Soviet-exploited Pan-Slavism. One Slav nation, it seemed, had been rewarded at the expense of its brother.

Lastly, although the transfer of territory was legalized by treaty, the somewhat dubious methods employed by the Russians warrant careful attention. The alleged plebiscite, for instance, was conducted without Czech participation. According to the *Soviet News* of July 2, 1945, the official Soviet view was as follows: "The population received an opportunity to express freely its desire concerning its own future. On November 26, 1944 [when the Czech Government was still in London] the first Conference of Transcarpathian Ukrainian People's Committees opened in Mukacevo [the capital of Ruthenia], attended by representatives of the whole country. Amid great enthusiasm the conference adopted a manifesto expressing the desire to unite the Transcarpathian Ukraine with the Soviet Ukraine. Following the manifesto, numerous meetings were held in towns and villages in which the population unanimously endorsed it."

This then was the plebiscite on which the legality of Soviet action was based. While her wartime allies were busy transferring armies and supplies from Europe to the Far East for their war against Japan, the

20 *Soviet News*, London, July 2, 1945.
21 Radio Moscow broadcast, November 6, 1945; reported in the *New York Times*, November 7, 1945.

Soviet Union quickly and efficiently consolidated Ruthenia into the Ukraine. Success apparently whetted the Russian appetite, for Communist action in Czechoslovakia and Central Europe was soon followed by even more pretentious designs in the Middle East.

CHAPTER 12

TURKEY

"The Soviet Government confirms its loyalty to the Montreux Convention, and assures the Turkish Government that it entertains no aggressive intention and claims in respect of the Straits. The Soviet Government . . . is prepared scrupulously to respect the territorial inviolability of the Turkish Republic."—Statement by the Soviet Government, August 10, 1941.

It is interesting to recall in connection with the above statement that only nine months before, the Soviet Union had arrived at an entirely different solution to this problem in conferences with Nazi Germany. At that time, a Secret Protocol of the proposed Four Power Pact between Germany, Italy, the USSR, and Japan had stated that the first three of these powers would "work in common toward the replacement of the Montreux Straits Convention by another convention" by which the "Soviet Union would be granted the right of unrestricted passage of its navy through the Straits at any time." No other nations except Black Sea powers, Germany and Italy were to exercise this right. Soviet Russia, moreover, had suggested that she also receive "a base for light naval and land forces on the Bosporus and the Dardanelles by means of a long-term lease."

At the Yalta Conference in 1945, the Soviet Government advanced proposals to the U.S. and Britain, regarding Turkey and the Straits, strikingly similar to those discussed with Germany in the autumn of 1940. The Big Three, however, arrived at no decision on the matter and agreed only that the problem should be considered at a subsequent conference.

So the issue was placed on the agenda at Potsdam. As had Germany and Italy previously, the U.S. and Britain agreed with the Soviet Union that the Montreux Convention should be revised. However, the Anglo-American combine did not go into as great detail as had the powers of the Rome-Berlin Axis. The Potsdam decision was in fact, very general in character: "The three Governments recognize that the con-

114

vention concluded at Montreux should be revised as failing to meet present-day conditions . . . the next step should be the subject of direct conversations between each of the three Governments and the Turkish Government."

The general character of the decision at Potsdam may well have reflected a certain Anglo-American suspicion of Soviet intentions as revealed in the months between Yalta and Potsdam. During this interval, the USSR had taken certain measures to alter the Turkish status quo to its own advantage. For instance, on March 20, 1945, the Soviet Information Bureau announced that the Soviet Government had informed Turkey of its wish to terminate the joint neutrality treaty of 1925. The terms of this treaty provided for the neutrality of one signatory in the event the other signatory became involved in war with a third party, and pledged further that neither party would attack, nor enter into any blocs, coalitions, or agreements against the other party. The reasons for the Soviet denunciation of this treaty, according to Molotov, were that "great changes had taken place, particularly during the Second World War", which required a new understanding.[1] On March 21, 1945, *Izvestiya* reported that it was "not in the interest of the two countries to extend the terms of an agreement concluded in a totally different situation." What is more, "it is clear that the Soviet-Turkish agreement calls for serious amendments."

The Soviet Government did not mention at the time what amendments it proposed. It was not until June 25, 1945, that a hint of the Russian demands became generally known. In an oral communication to the Turkish Foreign Minister, the Soviets stated that prerequisites for the re-establishment of the friendship treaty would include joint defense of the Straits, revision of the Montreux Convention, and cession of the Turkish areas of Kars and Ardahan.[2] This disturbing situation, it will be remembered, was all prior to Potsdam.

It was obvious that the Western powers had no intention of backing either the Soviet demand for Kars and Ardahan or that for joint defense bases on the Straits. The declaration at Potsdam was therefore purposely vague. Nor were the Turks, long antagonists of Russia, likely to accept peacefully any Soviet territorial demands. They were amenable to a partial revision of the Montreaux Convention, but that was all. By August 7, 1945, Istanbul even talked of war, hopeless as it would doubtless be, if the Soviet Government pushed its territorial demands.

[1] Soviet Information Bureau, March 20, 1945; *New York Times*, March 21, 1945.
[2] *Times*, London, June 25-28, 1945.

The USSR propaganda machine had been operating at near capacity for some time. Radio broadcasts from Soviet Armenia directed to Armenian refugees in Syria and Lebanon referred to the ill-treatment of Armenians by the Turks and called for the return to the Soviet Union of Armenian territories such as Kars and Ardahan.

Shortly thereafter, the propaganda machine of the Georgian Soviet Republic had also begun operating at full power. During the Three Power Foreign Minister's meeting in Moscow in December 1945, the intellectual efforts of two Georgian historians were published in *Izvestiya* and *Pravda*. Their studies were apparently designed to provide the legal and historical basis for a proposed USSR expansion into Turkey. "We appeal to world opinion about the situation of our ancient land taken by Turkey," the Georgian historians cried. "We are not talking about some small territorial dispute." (Like the Soviet-Armenian demand for Kars and Ardahan?) "This concerns the seized cradle of our people—a crime which has cut in two our living national body. The Georgian people must get back their land."[3]

The lands to which the vociferous Georgians referred were the Turkish areas of Artvin, Ardahan (which conflicted with the territorial desires of the Armenian Soviets), Oltu, Tortum, Ispir, Bayburt, Guemuesane, Giresun, and Trabzon. By way of illustration as to the extent of their demands, Trabzon was a relatively important port on the Black Sea nearly 100 miles away from the Soviet border and the largest city in that part of Turkey. The Georgian claims did not stop there, but demanded in addition that the Turks cede approximately 180 miles of their Black Sea coast up to the port of Giresun, with territory stretching inland to a depth of approximately 75 miles. The Georgian historians dismissed the fact that with the exception of Kars and Ardahan, the areas they claimed had been Turkish since the sixteenth century. The two exceptions, Kars and Ardahan, had been Tsarist Russia's for forty years. They had been ceded to the Russians by the Turks following the Russo-Turkish War of 1878, and remained Russian until the overthrow of the Tsar in World War I. Both provinces had then reverted to Turkish ownership under terms of the Brest-Litovsk Treaty,[4] subsequently reaffirmed in a 1921 treaty with Soviet Russia. In actual fact, however, the regions had been historically inhabited largely by Armenians and Georgians, but through dispersion

[3] For a full account see *Izvestiya* and *Pravda*, December 20, 1945; *New York Times*, December 21, 1945; *Soviet News*, London, December 22, 1945.

[4] Turkey was an ally of Germany during World War I, and thus benefited from the terms of the Treaty of Brest-Litovsk.

and often more violent means, there were few Armenians or Georgians in the areas as of 1945.

The historical reason for the claims by Georgia and Armenia—neither more nor less valid than would be a French claim to Quebec—were advanced at a time thought apropos by the Kremlin for planned Soviet aggrandizement. The basis, of course, was the Soviet multinational policy which in this case put the weight of the gigantic Soviet Union behind the nationalistic desires of little Armenia and Georgia. But against a resolute Turkey, however, Armenia and Georgia had little chance of receiving their desired territorial satisfaction unless the entire Soviet Union were willing to go to war. At this particular time the USSR was not willing to do so, and the demand consequently appeared likely to remain an unsettled source of friction between Turkey and Soviet Russia in all of their future relations.

Claims for the Turkish territory revealed another characteristic of Soviet diplomacy. To be sure, the Politburo must have realized that acquisition of the territories was at the time nearly impossible without war. Nevertheless, it instigated claims and demanded ownership, obviously hoping to satisfy the peculiar, contradictory, and newly-kindled nationalism of the Armenians and Georgians. This was perhaps an indication that the development of Soviet multinationalism and the resulting territorial aspirations of the Soviet Republics was possibly a monster that might escape the Kremlin as easily as it had many another imperialist government.

A second characteristic revealed in Soviet territorial claims on Turkey was that of advancing absolute maximum demands on the expectation that nothing was to be lost and at least something would be gained. The Kremlin had achieved enormous success with this method in relations with Hitler, Roosevelt, and Churchill, all of whom had initially accepted the maximum apparently without bothering to insist strongly on the minimum demands. In this case, the Soviet Union evidently assumed that its primary demands for control of the Straits would have a better chance of realization if at the same time claims were advanced for Kars, Ardahan, and northeastern Turkey. Subsequently if it appeared one of these claims could be realized by sacrificing another, then well and good. It was part of the much larger postwar Soviet strategy of applying expansionist pressure in several areas on the presumption that at least some of the several objectives would be realized.

The cities of Batum in Georgia and Erivan in Armenia were also of good use in the Soviet method of expansion. Here as elsewhere along the lengthy frontier important cities were located. Some day these cities might be considered so intolerably close to Turkey that their security would be greatly endangered, as was the case of Leningrad to Finland. The USSR would then have the necessary pretext for demanding a border adjustment to place these cities beyond the range of potential artillery bombardment. Moreover, the two cities served still another purpose. As long as a large part of the Turkish annual budget went toward defense, it would be nearly impossible to carry out the development plans of the late Kemal Ataturk. In the meantime, the regions across the border in Armenia and Georgia in general, and Batum and Erivan in particular, would continue to develop at a relatively fast pace. The improvements these cities possessed, few as they might be, were an attraction to the bordering populations in Turkey. As such, these people would supposedly be much more favorably inclined toward the ideas of the Soviet Union.

Strategically and economically the Turkish regions were naturally desirable acquisitions and clearly were on the Soviet blueprint for expansion. Since the Turks appeared most unlikely to attack the Soviet Union, the region was much more valuable to the Turks than to the Soviets as insurance against attack. The topography was mountainous and strategically excellent for purposes of defense.

Although Soviet demands for Turkish regions were greatly minimized from the beginning of 1946 onward, the nearly 300,000 people and at least 6,600 square miles of territory had become the object of a definite Soviet claim. There was good reason to believe that along the great Eurasian border axis of the USSR the pressure of aggrandizement would doubtless be applied again to Kars and Ardahan.

Far stronger than Kremlin demands for these Turkish provinces, however, was the Soviet insistence for adjustment of both the Montreaux Convention and other concessions relating to the Straits. Historically, Russia had always been confronted with Turkish control of the Bosporus and Dardanelles. It had been a long-standing and frustrating desire of the Russians not only to gain an unrestricted outlet to the Mediterranean, but at the same time to make the Black Sea a Russian lake inaccessible to vessels of other nations in time of war. The Tsars, however, had never quite succeeded in realizing either of these aims.

The Montreux Convention establishing the status of the Straits and to which the Soviet Union objected so strongly had been signed July 20, 1936. It replaced an earlier post-World War I agreement providing for the demilitarization of the Bosporus, the Sea of Marmora, and certain islands in the Aegean. The earlier agreement also established a Straits Commission responsible to the League of Nations and provided an international guarantee for freedom of navigation in the Straits and security for the demilitarized zone.

In 1936, Turkey requested a meeting of the treaty powers in order to abrogate the demilitarization clauses. The idea was favorably received by all signatory powers except Italy, and it was subsequently agreed at a conference in Montreux, Switzerland, that Turkey could remilitarize the Straits. In addition, with the exception of Black Sea powers, limits were imposed on the aggregate tonnage of warships allowed in transit through the Straits at any one time and on the type and maximum tonnage of warships of non-riparian powers to be admitted to the Black Sea. Furthermore, it was agreed that in time of war no large fleet of a non-riparian state could enter the Black Sea except on the invitation of the Turkish Government. The Montreux Convention was then signed by ten powers including the USSR.

The traditional Russian aim has been to keep the Straits closed to worships of other powers while leaving them open for Russian warships to go in and out of the Mediterranean. This idea could be realized only by means of an international convention or by direct possession. In 1915, Russia had been promised what amounted to direct possession by the Allied Powers, but, having succumbed to revolution and defeat before the 1918 Armistice, had not achieved this objective. In 1946 the Russians sought to combine the idea of direct possession with international convention.

Early in August of 1946, the USSR presented a note to Turkey proposing that a new regime be established in the Straits on the following principles:

"1. The Straits should always be open for the passage of merchant ships of all countries.

"2. The Straits should always be open for the passage of warships of the Black Sea Powers.

"3. The passage of warships of non-Black Sea Powers through the Straits is not to be permitted, except in cases specially provided for.

"4. Responsibility for establishing a regime for these Straits, the sole sea route leading out of and into the Black Sea, must lie with Turkey and the other Black Sea Powers.

"5. Turkey and the Soviet Union as the Powers most interested in and capable of ensuring the freedom of merchant shipping and security in the Straits, shall jointly organize the defence of the Straits to prevent their use by other States for purposes hostile to the Black Sea Powers."[5]

5 *Soviet Weekly*, London, August 22, 1946.

In their reply, the Turks agreed in principle to the first three of the Soviet proposals, but objected to points four and five. A new regime composed only of Black Sea Powers would lead to disregard of the interests of other Powers, the Turkish note said. Moreover, it maintained that joint defense of the Straits by Turkey and the Soviet Union would be incompatible with the sovereign rights of Turkey and destroy her security.[6]

The Kremlin's reply to the Turkish note elaborated more fully on the reasoning of point four. "The Soviet Government," the note read, "desires to call the Turkish Government's attention to the special position of the Black Sea as a land-locked sea." This means, said the note, that the Straits are "a sea route leading only to the shores of a limited number of powers, namely to the shores of the several Black Sea powers. It is perfectly natural therefore, that the Soviet Union and other Black Sea powers should be chiefly concerned about settling the Black Sea Straits regime, and that their position in this case cannot be compared to that of other powers." Furthermore, the note continued, the Straits can't be compared to international sea routes such as Gibralter and Suez which are main sea routes, because the Straits lead merely to the land-locked Black Sea.

To the fifth point, which Turkey had rejected on the grounds that joint defense was incompatible with her sovereignty, the USSR stated: The rejection by Turkey was "before it had even listened to any concrete considerations on this matter, and without even trying to consider jointly the relevant proposal made by the USSR." Furthermore, the Turkish Government "finds it possible to express suspicions which are utterly groundless and, moreover are incompatible with the dignity of the Soviet Union," concluded the note of the Soviet Foreign Ministry.[7]

The Turkish reply to the second Soviet note rejected the idea of any bilateral Straits control between Russia and her satellites on one hand and Turkey on the other. Her position both on the Black Sea and on the Mediterranean, said Turkey, made it impossible to agree that only Black Sea powers should control the Straits. Moreover, in that the administration of the Straits had been established by signatories of the Montreux Convention, it would be impossible to arrange this condition without the express consent of these signatory powers. Furthermore, Turkey again insisted that in regard to joint defense it would be incompatible "with the unchangeable rights of the sovereignty of

6 *New York Times*, August 25, 1946.
7 *Soviet Weekly*, London, October 3, 1946.

Turkey and with its security which cannot permit any restrictions."[8]

The Turks subsequently suggested that defense of the Straits could be better entrusted to the United Nations than to a joint agreement between their country and the USSR. This was the last of the note exchanges. The unchanged Montreux Convention continued to govern the administration of the Straits.

Soviet Russia had based her contention for control of the Straits on security. USSR security, however, did not warrant the establishment of defense bases on Turkish soil. Turkey, obviously aware of what had happened to the Baltic States under such an arrangement and cognizant of Soviet tactics as only a neighboring state can be, felt well justified in rejecting the Soviet demands. As for establishing a governing Straits regime composed of only the Black Sea powers, Turkey had little enthusiasm. In all but name the other Black Sea countries were as much a part of the USSR as Soviet Armenia. The result of such an agreement would be that Turkey, through whose territory ran the Straits, would have a minority voice in their control, a situation naturally unthinkable to the Turks.

In this incident then, the historical Russian ambition to control the Straits was once more frustrated. It was apparent, however, that Soviet intentions went considerably beyond control of the Straits; from all indications, the USSR merely intended to use such control for creating a subservient Turkey. This fact was evident when Soviet Russia refused to negotiate on the first three conditions of her August 1946 note, which Turkey and other interested nations had actually accepted in principle. It was even more evident in an age of air power because the USSR with airfields in a neighboring People's Democracy could doubtless control the air and thus effectively control the entrance of any hostile warships into the Black Sea.

Through all of Soviet Russia's postwar demands, however, Turkey remained territorially undamaged, while the aims and ambitions of the Soviet Union toward Turkey and the Straits were clearly revealed in their postwar perspective. Methods of aggrandizement used on other nations with considerable success failed against Turkey. Future Soviet success would require the use of much harsher means.

In the meantime, to the east of Turkey, the Minindel[9] was utilizing a different method of aggrandizement which came far closer to success than the Turkish failure, but which brought world attention and resistance to the Soviet plan of territorial aggrandizement.

[8] *New York Times*, October 21, 1946.

[9] The Narkomindel, or Commissariat of Foreign Affairs, was changed in 1946 to the Minindel, or Ministry of Foreign Affairs.

CHAPTER 13

IRAN

"Our armed forces, closely rallied around the Soviet Government, are a reliable bastion of the Soviet Union's foreign policy."—Marshall Bulganin, Red Army Day 1948.

Following Soviet Russia's entry into the war, German activity in Iran was intensified to the point where it presented a grave threat to the southern flank of USSR defenses. Consequently, for purposes of security, the Soviet Union and Great Britain occupied the Kingdom of Iran in August 1941. Both nations found it convenient to pledge their respect for the independence and sovereignty of that country and proclaimed that they would withdraw their troops as soon as the German danger had passed.

The Soviet occupation was based on a valid treaty obligation contained in Article VI of the Soviet-Iranian Treaty of February 26, 1921. Until 1941, however, the Soviets had never invoked the particular clause which allowed them to send troops into northern Iranian territory. But the war situation was so pressing in August of that year that the Kremlin was compelled to act, and act quickly. The basis for Soviet action was officially that "Iran might be utilized by elements hostile both to the USSR and to Iran itself, and that these elements might attempt to transform Iran into a base for attacks on the USSR."[1] Therefore, the USSR was acting in accordance with the Treaty of 1921, which stated:

"Both High Contracting Parties are agreed that, in the event of attempts on the part of third countries by means of armed intervention to effect a policy of conquest on Persian territory, or to transform the territory of Persia into a base for military operations against Russia, and if this shall involve a threat to the frontiers of the Russian Socialist

---

[1] Note of the Soviet Government to the Government of Iran, August 25, 1941. *Soviet Foreign Policy During the Patriotic War, Documents and Materials,* vol. I, translated by Andrew Rothstein, (London 1945), p. 89.

Federal Soviet Republic or its allies, and if the Persian Government after warning received from the Russian Soviet Government [then the latter] will have the right to introduce its troops into Persian territory, for the purpose of taking the necessary military measures in the interests of self-defense. Upon the elimination of such danger, the Soviet Government undertakes to withdraw its troops from the territory of Persia."

Iran, of course, as in no position to resist either the USSR or Britain and so was forced to accept the Allied occupation. The Iranian pro-German monarch, Riza Shah Pahlevi, abdicated and was succeeded by his son Riza Mohammed Pahlevi on September 17, 1941.

In line with this new state of conditions, three events took place during the following two years that were to have particular bearing on events after the end of hostilities in Europe. The first of these was a tripartite treaty of alliance signed by Britain, USSR, and Iran on January 29, 1942, under which the first two powers agreed to "jointly and severally respect the territorial integrity, sovereignty and political independence of Iran." Britain and the USSR were, in addition, granted the right to maintain land, sea, and air forces on Iranian territory, but promised to withdraw them "not later than six months after all hostilities between the Allied Powers and Germany and her associates" were "suspended."

The second event happened a few months later, on September 9, 1943, when Iran considered it to her benefit to declare war on Germany. As a result, she shortly after became a signatory of the United Nations Declaration. That Iran thus became one of the United Nations was later to be the salvation of her territorial integrity.

Finally, at Teheran on December 1, 1943, Roosevelt, Churchill, and Stalin issued a "Declaration of the Three Powers Concerning Iran." This document stated that the Three Powers were "at one with the Government of Iran in their desire for the maintenance of the independence, sovereignty and territorial integrity of Iran."

It was not until October of 1944, that the Soviet Government began to show any official interest in capitalizing on Iran's plight. On the 10th of that month a Tass dispatch revealed that a Soviet mission was negotiating with the Iranian Government for an oil concession in the Azerbaijan region of northern Iran, somewhat similar to the British concession in southern Iran. But a week later, there were indications that the negotiations had not gone according to Soviet plan. Iran had refused to consider USSR proposals until the end of the war. The Soviet press immediately began sharp attacks on the "disloyal and unfriendly attitude" of the Iranian Government. According to the official Soviet view, this was "tantamount to a refusal", and worked "towards a worsening of relations" between the two countries.[2] It was pointed out to the skeptical Iranians that the Soviet oil concessions would provide employment for the population, further the development of agriculture in the districts near the oil concessions, enable Iranians to train as geological engineers in the USSR, and provide scores of other benefits. The Iranian Government, claimed the Soviet spokesman, could not "put forward a single convincing reason" why it should not grant concessions immediately. What is more, the Kremlin alleged subsequently, the USSR already possessed a legal basis for the development of oil in Iran since a certain pre-Soviet Georgian named Khoshtaria had held valid concession rights for Iranian oil exploitation which were automatically transferred to the USSR from Tsarist Russia.[3] Nevertheless, the Soviets evidently did not regard Khoshtaria's claims as valid enough to begin operations without the consent of the Iranian Government.

Following the end of hostilities in Europe, Iran requested Britain, the U. S.,[4] and the USSR to withdraw their troops from Iranian territory in accordance with terms of the treaties and declarations to this effect. Four months after this request in September 1945, doubts arose in London and Washington as to whether the Red Army intended to leave Iran. It was reported on September 3 that Soviet authorities had prevented Iranian police from moving north to quell disturbances instigated by the Communist-front "Tudeh" Party. Moreover, telegraphic communications between Teheran and several parts of the northern provinces occupied by the Red Army had been cut. The Teheran Government immediately expressed open concern for its territorial integrity.[5] In London, Foreign Secretary Ernest Bevin was prompted to notify Molotov that, according to the 1942 Anglo-Soviet-Iranian Treaty, Britain and the USSR had agreed to withdraw their troops six months after the ending of hostilities. Figuring from VJ Day on September 2, 1945, the withdrawal date would accordingly be March 2, 1946. Molotov replied to the British note in a tone of indignation. "I would ask you to bear in mind that the Soviet Government attaches

[2] Statement by Deputy People's Commissar for Foreign Affairs Kavtaradze at a press conference in Teheran, October 24, 1944, Tass. *Soviet Foreign Policy*, vol. II, pp. 164-6.

[3] *New York Times*, May 20, 1945.

[4] The U. S. had taken part in the occupation of Iran to assist in the operation of the wartime supply route between the Persian Gulf and the USSR.

[5] *New York Times*, September 3, 1945.

exceptional importance to strict fulfillment of obligations undertaken."[6]

There appeared to be considerable doubt, however, as to the party with whom the Soviet Union had contracted obligations, for on November 9, 1945, it was noted that the Red Army had been greatly reinforced in northern Iran, and only nine days later a revolt broke out against the Iranian Government in the Soviet-occupied province of Azerbaijan. On the following day, November 19, the Iranian Ambassador in Washington, Hussein Ala, charged that the revolt was "engineered" by the Soviet Union.[7]

Greatly disturbed by the implications of the revolt, the U. S. dispatched a note to the USSR on November 27, proposing that the U. S., U. K., and USSR withdraw all troops from Iran by January 1, 1946. The Russians replied two days later that they saw no grounds for advancing the evacuation date, and at the same time, denied that the Red Army hand hindered the movement of Iranian military forces seeking to quell the revolt.[8]

In spite of Minindel denials of Soviet interference, it was announced by the Moscow radio on December 16, 1945, that a National Government of Iranian Azerbaijan had been formed in Tabriz, provincial capital of the region. The leader of the government, according to the Moscow radio, was Jaafar Pishevari, reputed head of the Democratic Party of Azerbaijan, an outgrowth of the Iranian Communist-front Tudeh Party, which had instigated the revolt a month earlier. Pishevari had been involved in a Bolshevik effort to establish an Iranian Soviet regime at Resht in Gilan Province twenty-five years previously, and had been a refugee in Russia until the Red Army occupied northern Iran in 1941.

Shortly after the Moscow announcement, Iran attempted to dispatch 1,500 troops to reassert Iranian sovereignty over the disaffected area, but they were prohibited from entering northern Iran by 30,000 Red Army troops. The Soviet justification for this interference was that the 1,500 ill-equipped Iranians presented a grave danger to the 30,000 well-equipped Soviets.

Secretary of State Byrnes, who at the time was in Moscow at a Foreign Minister's Conference, told Stalin that the Soviet reasoning was difficult to comprehend. Stalin then outlined what he called "the pertinent facts" in the matter. The Baku oil fields in the south of Rus-

[6] Note of the USSR to the Government of the United Kingdom, September 20, 1945. New York Times, April 4, 1946.

[7] New York Times, November 9, 19, 20, 1945.

[8] Ibid., November 28, 30, 1945.

sia, he said to Byrnes, were close to the Iranian border and this created a special problem. These oil fields had to be safeguarded against any possible hostile action by Iran against the USSR, and no confidence could be placed in the Iranian Government in Teheran. Saboteurs, said Stalin, might be sent to the Baku oil fields to set them on fire. In any case, the Soviet Government had a right to maintain troops in Iran until March 15, 1946 and did not want to withdraw before that date. (The U. S. and U. K. had assumed March 2, 1946 to be the deadline.) At that time, Stalin continued, it would be possible to examine the situation and see whether it would be feasible to withdraw the Red Army. He reminded Byrnes that by terms of the 1921 treaty the USSR had the right to maintain troops in northern Iran if there was a danger from an outside source. But the Soviet Union, concluded Stalin, had no designs, territorial or otherwise, against Iran and would withdraw its troops as soon as it felt secure about the Baku oil fields.[9]

Needless to say, Byrnes was hardly reassured by Stalin's attitude. Nor was the Iranian Government reassured by Soviet actions. Consequently, on January 19, 1946, at a meeting of the newly-formed United Nations Security Council, Iran charged that a situation existed which endangered world peace: "Owing to interference by the Soviet Union, through the medium of their officials and armed forces, in the internal affairs of Iran, a situation has arisen which may lead to international friction. In accordance with Article 33 of the Charter of the United Nations, the Iranian Government has repeatedly tried to negotiate with the Government of the Soviet Union but has met with no success."[10]

The USSR, of course, "categorically" refuted the Iranian charges. The presence of troops on Iranian territory is quite legitimate, said the Soviets, and is based not only on the Soviet-Iranian Treaty of 1921, but on the Soviet-British-Iranian Treaty of 1942. "The events in Iranian Azerbaijan have no connection with the presence there of Soviet troops," the note asserted. "These events are of an exclusively Iranian and internal nature. What is happening in northern Iran reflects the aspiration of the population of northern Iran for national autonomy within the limits of the Iranian State, and the achievement of the wishes of the local population." Moreover, continued the Soviet note, "anti-democratic and pogrom activity hostile to the Soviet Union, conducted by reactionary forces in Iran and supported by certain influential Iranian groups drawn from the ruling circles and the police

[9] James F. Byrnes, *Speaking Frankly, op. cit.,* pp. 118-21.
[10] *United Nations Journal of the Security Council,* January 24, 1946, p. 13.

authorities creates for the Azerbaijan Soviet Socialist Republic and for Baku a danger of organized hostile actions, diversionist acts, and so forth. Such a situation cannot be tolerated." Moreover, the Soviet statement concluded the matter, was of no concern to the Security Council, and should be settled solely by bi-lateral negotiations between the two countries.[11] While denying that the USSR had had anything whatsoever to do with the Azerbaijan revolt, the Soviet reply simultaneously seemed to justify and confirm Soviet interference. The U. N. Security Council, proceeding cautiously, asked the two governments to settle their differences by negotiation, but requested the parties to inform the Council of any results achieved, and in the meantime retained the right to request information on the progress of the negotiations.

However, direct negotiations between the two countries were unsuccessful. During a February and early March meeting between Iranian Premier Ahmad Ghavam and Stalin, the USSR advanced three principal demands: First, that troops be maintained in certain sections of Iran for an indefinite period. Second, that Iran recognize the autonomous regime of Azerbaijan, in return for which the Soviet Union offered to take steps to arrange that the Prime Minister of Azerbaijan would bear the title of Governor General in relation to the Teheran Government; moreover that Azerbaijan would have no Ministry of War or Foreign Affairs, and that thirty per cent of the Azerbaijan revenue would be paid the Teheran Government. Third, that a joint Soviet-Iranian oil company—51 per cent Soviet and 49 per cent Iranian —be formed to exploit oil in the northern part of the country.[12]

Ghavam sought to postpone a definite answer to the Soviet demands until after March 2, when the Soviets had pledged to withdraw their troops. But March 2 passed and the Red Army still gave no indication of returning to Soviet soil. Britain and the U.S. immediately sent sharp notes to the Minindel, but received no answer to their protests. On the contrary, Red Army troops poured across the Iranian frontier with two columns fanning out toward Iraq and Turkey and one column sweeping within a few miles of the Iranian capital, Teheran.[13]

By this time Soviet aggression was taken very seriously in Washington and London. New notes demanding an explanation of Red Army movements were sent to Moscow, but without result. On March 18, the Iranian Government filed a formal notice with the United Nations Secretary General that a dispute had arisen between it and the

[11] Security Council, *op. cit.*, pp. 17-19. Also *Soviet Weekly,* January 31, 1946.
[12] *New York Times,* March 28, 1946.
[13] Department of State press release, March 12, 1944.

USSR "the continuance of which is likely to endanger the maintenance of international peace and security." The Soviet Union, Iran announced, had violated the treaty of 1942, the Teheran Declaration, and the United Nations Charter.[14]

Soviet Russia now sought without success to postpone the March 25 meeting of the Security Council until April 10. During this proposed two-week delay, the USSR evidently had hoped to bring about a decided change in the attitude of the Teheran Government, or perhaps a change in the Government itself. There were in fact strong indications that some progress toward this end had taken place when on March 24, 1946, the day before the scheduled meeting of the Security Council, the USSR announced that according to an agreement with Iran Red Army troops would be withdrawn within six weeks "unless unforeseen circumstances arise."[15]

When the Security Council met on March 26-27, the Soviet delegate, Andrei Gromyko, sought to have the matter removed from consideration on the grounds that the purported agreement of the day before, pledging Soviet removal of troops from Iran within six weeks, had solved the problem. With no information on the alleged agreement other than Gromyko's, the Security Council rejected Soviet Russia's request and asked the Iranian delegate to state his case. However, before the Iranian could speak, the Soviet representative again suggested a delay until April 10. This suggestion too was refused. At this point, to the obvious concern of other member nations, Gromyko walked out of the Security Council hearings, stating that under the circumstances he could not remain. Immediate fears that the USSR was leaving the United Nations were, however, unfounded. The Soviets continued to take part in all UN functions other than the debates on Iran.[16]

Hussein Ala, the Iranian delegate, then set forth his country's case. He knew of no agreement between his country and the USSR, secret or otherwise, with respect to the matter before the Council; to the best of his knowledge, the Iranian declared, the Teheran Government had rejected all the Soviet proposals.[17]

The Security Council then asked that Iran and Russia reveal the present state of the negotiations for the removal of Red Army troops and indicate whether the reported withdrawal of the Red Army was conditional upon other subjects.[18]

[14] Security Council, *op. cit.*, pp. 351-53.
[15] *New York Times*, March 25, 1946; Security Council, *op. cit.*, p. 353, p. 366-9.
[16] *Ibid.*, pp. 381-420.
[17] *Ibid.*, pp. 424-9.
[18] *Ibid.*, pp. 433-45.

On April 3 the Soviet Union replied that withdrawal of troops had commenced on March 24 and would be completed within six weeks. The other subject, said the Soviet Government, was not connected with troop withdrawal since the matter of oil concessions had been raised in 1944 independently of the evacuation question.[19]

At the same time, the Iranian delegate revealed that Soviet interference in Iran's internal affairs was still continuing. On March 24, he claimed the Soviet Ambassador had presented three memoranda to Iran, the first of which dealt with the withdrawal of troops, the second with the formation of a Soviet-controlled oil-development company, and the third with Azerbaijan autonomy. He added that on March 27 the Soviet Ambassador had stated orally that if agreement were reached in connection with the second and third subjects, no "unforeseen circumstances" would arise in connection with the evacuation of troops. The Iranian delegate then asserted that if the Soviet Government would give unconditional assurances of the evacuation of its troops by May 6 then Iran would not press further for consideration of the matter by the Security Council at that time, provided that the matter remained on the Council agenda.[20]

This decision was of course welcomed by the Security Council, which immediately decided to defer further discussion on the subject until May 6, the day that Soviet Russia had finally agreed to withdraw her troops from Iran. If Russia's performances did not match her promise, warned the Security Council mildly, the matter would be opened for more discussion at once. Only one member, Hodgson of Australia, rightfully maintained that this did not meet the challenge presented, and refused to approve the Council's resolution.[21]

On April 5, the same day that the Council had resolved to wait-and-see, the Soviet Union announced that a treaty had been signed with Iran. This instrument provided first for the evacuation of Red Army troops from Iran by May 6, 1946; second, for the formation of a joint Soviet-Iranian oil company subject to the approval of the Iranian Parliament within seven months from March 24, 1946 (supposedly a more equitable arrangement than a Russian oil concession); and third, for the improvement of conditions in Azerbaijan—"an internal affair" said the treaty—in accordance with existing laws.[22]

Now that the matter was settled, said the Soviets, it should be removed from the Council agenda. Iran subsequently seconded the Soviet

[19] Security Council, *op. cit.*, pp. 451.
[20] *Ibid.*, pp. 451-3.
[21] *Ibid.*, pp. 462-4.
[22] Soviet *News*, April 6, 1946.

suggestion.[23] This time, however, the Council displayed a surprisingly firm attitude and refused to withdraw the subject from discussion.[24] On May 6, the day by which all Soviet troops were to be evacuated from Iran, the Iranian representatives told the Council he had no way of knowing whether Soviet troops had departed in that his government did not exercise authority in the province of Azerbaijan because of continued Soviet interference.[25] His statement was most revealing as to the real situation but embarrassing to his government, which immediately ordered that he was not to appear again before the Council. On May 21, however, the Teheran Government was able to announce that "no trace whatever" remained of Soviet troops in Iran, including Azerbaijan. Two days later, the Soviet radio confirmed this statement by reporting that full evacuation of Soviet troops had been completed on May 9. Although the Iranian representative, contrary to his previous instructions, told the Council on May 22 that it could not ignore the fact that Azerbaijan, an integral part of Iran, was not under the authority of the Iranian Government, the Council passed a resolution adjourning discussion of the subject "until a date in the near future."[26] The "near future", however, turned out to be the following December.

After the withdrawal of the Red Army from Iran the Iranian Central Government apparently gained a great deal of internal strength during the summer and fall of 1946. Initially it had been necessary to welcome Soviet-sponsored autonomous Azerbaijan back into the nominal control of the Teheran Government. This action had been taken with forced good feeling in June.[27] During the months that followed a growing distaste developed among Iranians for the Communist-front Tudeh Party and its supporters in autonomous Azerbaijan.[28] In September, southern tribes, demanding a strong anti-Tudeh policy, revolted. In October, Premier Ghavam decided that his position was secure enough to form a new ministry without Tudeh members. And in November, Ghavam announced that national elections would be held in Azerbaijan under the supervision of Iranian Government forces.[29]

The last measure was of considerable concern to the Soviet Union.

[23] Security Council, *op. cit.*, pp. 489-91; 497-500; 516.

[24] *Ibid.*, p. 597.

[25] *Ibid.*, p. 634.

[26] *Ibid.*, p. 711-14.

[27] *New York Times*, June 12, 1946.

[28] *United States in World Affairs, 1945-47*, Council on Foreign Relations, J. C. Campbell ed. (New York 1947) p. 556, September 22, 1946.

[29] *Ibid.*, p. 556, Oct. 19, 1946.

Realizing that its position in Azerbaijan would be weakened by the presence of Iranian troops to supervise elections, on December 6, 1946, the Soviet Ambassador in Teheran advised the Ghavam Government not to send troops into Azerbaijan for fear that they might cause an incident. This advice was immediately passed on to the world press much to the annoyance of the Politburo. In spite of the Soviet warning, Iranian troops advanced into Azerbaijan on December 10, and captured Tabriz, the Azerbaijan capital, the following day. At this point the "democratic militia" of the Tudeh group was ordered to capitulate and welcome the Iranian Army. This was the last act of Pishevari and the Soviet-sponsored regime before they fled across the border to the Azerbaijan Soviet Republic.

The Soviet press immediately denounced the Iranian Government's act as one in complete disregard of international treaty obligations, as well as dishonest, infamous, and "envied by any band of Fascists." The reactionary U.S. and Britain were censured as being behind the move to crush Azerbaijan independence, and Tabriz was described as being "like an occupied city" with "national memorials destroyed, editorial offices ransacked," and "bodies of murdered democrats lying in the streets."[30]

From all indications, the Soviet regime in Azerbaijan had become tremendously unpopular with the local population.[31] To save it would have necessitated strong measures by the USSR and risked a serious clash with the western powers. From that moment on, Iran, even though a weak border state, was to assert an increasing amount of independence from Soviet influence.

Even the proposed joint oil company never came into existence. Doubtless because of Premier Ghavam's shrewdness, the agreement was not presented to the Miajlis (Parliament) until the autumn of 1947, and it then met with great dissatisfaction in that body. Subsequently, it was rumored that to show its displeasure at the Iranian move, the Soviet Government planned to take the matter before the United Nations.[32] However in view of the Kremlin's past performance there, this strategm would doubtless have enjoyed little chance of success.

Iran's greatest fear for the future arose from the treaty of 1921. As long as this agreement existed, the Soviet Union maintained the

[30] *Soviet News*, December 28, 1946.

[31] Archie Roosevelt Jr., "The Kurdish Republic of Mahabad" *The Middle East Journal*, July 1947, pp. 266-7.

[32] *New York Times*, September 28, 1947.

right to occupy the northern portions of Iran, and hence to exert powerful influence on the rest of the country. Even if Iran denounced the treaty, the Soviets could assert that abrogation depended on mutual consent of both parties.

Actually, the principal deterrent to Soviet aggression in Iran was the possibility of conflict with a perhaps weakened but nevertheless resolute Britain in turn supported by the United States. Penetration, even if not physically farther than Azerbaijan, and establishment of a subservient government in Teheran, would have extended the Soviet sphere of influence to the Persian Gulf, and would also have outflanked Turkey and British positions in the Middle East, including Arabia. Such a situation would be extremely difficult for the British to accept. The statement of President Truman on April 6, 1946, that "the Near and Middle East might become an area of intense rivalry between outside powers" which in turn could erupt into sudden conflict, was all too true.[33]

It will be remembered that Persia and the warm waters of the Persian Gulf have long been a focus of Russian policy. Both the armies of Peter the Great and Catherine the Great invaded the country. Considerably later, in 1907, there emerged an agreement with Britain whereby Russian influence was to be predominant in the north, British influence predominant in the south, with the middle area to serve as a buffer between the two powers. In 1920, the Bolsheviks had attempted to establish a Soviet government in the northern district of Gilan, but had failed because of the weakness of the Red Army. It was not until two decades later that the true desires of the Kremlin were finally revealed. As the proposed Four Power Pact of 1940 between the Axis and the USSR proclaimed: "The center of the aspirations of the Soviet Union is recognized as that area south of Batum and Baku in the general direction of the Persian Gulf." Hitler had thought that by encouraging Soviet expansion in that direction southeastern Europe would be left free for German territorial aggrandizement. In any case the Soviet aspiration was neither recognized nor realized, and within a year the USSR and Germany were at war with each other.

During the course of hostilities it became apparent to the Kremlin that the end of the war would terminate the Russian occupation of Iran and, unless something were done, that the historic as well as the professed Soviet desire for predominant influence as far south as the Persian Gulf would have to wait until some unknown future date. Although Communist theory maintained that time was on the side of

[33] *New York Times,* April 7, 1946.

the USSR and that the Soviet Union could wait patiently for the inevitable disintegration of the capitalist imperalist world, it was at the same moment opportunistic. There was a definite opportunity for the Kremlin to gain control of Iran at the end of the war. And with Iran would come a stentorian voice in the affairs of the Near and Middle East.

Once again that "reliable bastion of Soviet foreign policy" the Red Army, played an indispensable role. It served to support the Soviet plan for control of Iran which actually began when Moscow demanded oil concessions in the Iranian north. When the Iranians hedged in regard to the proposed concessions, the USSR retained the Red Army in Azerbaijan and applied added pressure to the "unfriendly reactionary regime" in Teheran.

The attempted Soviet aggrandizement was based once again on the multinational character of the Soviet Union. In this case, the Kremlin used the Azerbaijan Soviet Socialist Republic to further its ends. Azerbaijanis, it seemed, lived on either side of the Soviet-Iranian border, but in the USSR Soviet multinationalism allowed them to develop their own language and cultural traditions. Moreover, Soviet policy had provided the Azerbaijanis with some material improvements which, even though limited, were a tremendous attraction to people who had next to none. The Soviets, in short, exploited the unfortunate condition of the Iranian Azerbaijanis—a condition which the Teheran Government had done little to improve—as one pretext for USSR intervention. The Iranian Azerbaijanis had long been loyal to the Teheran Government, but they had legitimate unanswered grievances which the Communists turned to their own ends. This exploitation was engineered by Iranian Communist refugees and by the kindred Azerbaijanis in the Soviet Republic to the north.[34] These people formed the nucleus of the Democratic Party of Azerbaijan, an offshoot of Iran's Tudeh Party. These two organizations, supported by the Red Army, formed the mouthpiece and organizational structure of Soviet ambitions in

---

[34] The leaders in this group were either Russian-born or had close political affiliations with USSR. They included, beside Premier Pishevari: Mohammed Biriya, educated in Russia and Minister of Education in Azerbaijan; Dr. Salamollah Javid, Minister of the Interior, a Communist active in the 1919-20 agitation for uniting Azerbaijan with the USSR and Governor General of the autonomous regime; Sadiq Padegan, born in Russia and chairman of the Central Committee of the Azerbaijan Democratic Party; M. Adalat, member of the Russian Communist Party in Baku, and founder of the Democratic Party in Azerbaijan; and lastly General Danishiyan, Commander-in-Chief of the Democrat Army who spoke broken Turkish, knew no Persian and could speak, read and write Russian and only Russian. (See below.)

Iran. Originally the Tudeh, the parent organization, claimed that it had no connection whatsoever with the Communist Party and that it received no assistance from the USSR. However, the Tudeh followed the Communist line with undeviating consistency during its entire existence and never once did its ideas contradict the aims pursued by the USSR.[35]

It is interesting to note, however, that although the Tudeh followed the Soviet line without exception, neither it nor the USSR ever openly advocated annexation of Iranian Azerbaijan by Soviet Azerbaijan. Assuming that Soviet tactics in Iran would have paralleled similar tactics elsewhere, this action would logically have been the next step. The government of autonomous Azerbaijan suffered a heavy blow when the Red Army withdrew in May 1946, and thus was never in a position to advocate Soviet affiliation. The professed desire of the Tudeh, the Democrats of Azerbaijan, and the USSR was for an autonomous Azerbaijan within the framework of the Iranian nation. Excellent reasons underlay this desire. The Azerbaijan Democratic Party had demanded representation in the Iranian Parliament by one-third of the total membership for the obvious purpose of exerting ever-increasing control in the Government of Iran. By so doing, the Soviet could continue to expand their postwar sphere of domination by creating a Soviet satellite within the existing federal structure of a foreign state. Their obvious purpose was to increase the international representation of the Soviet Union. For instance, even though the USSR is represented in the United Nations by three Soviet republics, few people have adhered to the fiction that the Ukraine or Byelorussia are sovereign; nevertheless there are those who believe this to be so of the "People's Democracies" in Eastern Europe, and even of the Mongolian regime in Asia. The Politburo has obviously been more interested in the new indirect "friendly neighbor" aggrandizement than in the straight territorial acquisition of 1939-1940.

Although this indirect aggression did not succeed there remains the possibility of demanding the reunion of all Azerbaijanis in the same way that the USSR demanded the reunion of all Ukrainians, Byelorussians, etc. In the case of Iran this method can be worked with more than just the kindred Azerbaijanis. The USSR can even exploit Persian nationalism through the small group of ethnically similar Tajiks and

35 Evidence to this effect may be found in an article by George Lenczowski, "The Communist Movement in Iran", *The Middle East Journal*, January 1947, pp. 29-45; Edwin Muller, "Behind the Scenes in Azerbaijan", *American Mercury*, June 1946; *New York Times*, April 12, May 15, 1946; *Washington Post*, December 12, 1945 and April 6, 11, 12, 1946.

their Soviet Republic. Although not bordering on Iran, the Soviet Tajiks or Persians have been used to represent the true voice of all Persians and Tajikistan has often been proclaimed the center of Persian culture. In addition to the Tajiks, the Armenian Soviet Republic borders Iran in the northwest. The Armenians too might demand that their brothers in Iran be liberated from Persian oppression. The same situation is even more true in the east where the Soviet Union might claim that another group, the Iranian Turkmen, live under the foreign flag of Iran while the Soviet Turkmenians and their Soviet Republic support a glowing national culture.

The USSR can also use to good avail its modern cities conveniently located along the long southern border. Baku, in Soviet Azerbaijan, is portrayed as the magnetic capital of Azerbaijan culture and development. Fortunately for Iran, it is located a sufficient distance from the border so that no territorial revisions are necessary to safeguard it from enemy artillery fire. In regard to the Turkmen Soviet Republic, however, the Iranians are less fortunate. Ashkhabad, the relatively modern capital of this area, with its streetcars and new buildings, is only a few miles from the Iranian border, a situation which someday might well be considered intolerable for the safety of the USSR.

Although the immediate postwar plan for expansion into Iran was frustrated, Soviet attention has continued and doubtless will continue to focus on this section of Asia—especially with the increasing difficulty of aggrandizement in Europe.

In some respects the USSR owed its Azerbaijan failure to the unwanted publicity received in the UN Security Council, and the resulting pressure to withdraw its troops from Azerbaijan. In other respects, the Soviet Union retreated under British pressure. The Near and Middle East were still regarded as vital by Britain and any attempt of the USSR to change the status quo would probably have resulted in a serious conflict. Soviet intrigue and Soviet designs however were not confined solely to Iran. Other approaches were used throughout the war and after by the Russians in an attempt to reach the Persian Gulf and to outflank their British ally—all in accord with a fundamental technique of Soviet expansion: to wait patiently and be ready for the inevitable opportunity to present itself. Time, say Soviet leaders, will see the realization of all their aims.

CHAPTER 14

THE NEAR AND MIDDLE EAST:KURDISTAN
AND AFGHANISTAN

"If I cannot do by might, I'll do by slight. If I dare not attack my enemy openly, I'll do him an injury in a private and clandestine way."—James Kelly, "Scottish Proverbs," 1721.

Exploitation of nationalism has been a basic tenet of Soviet expansionist policy. The Near and Middle East has presented a field ripe for development. There are numerous backward, subjected, persecuted minorities in this area and in all of them stirs the unsmashed atom of self-determination. A multinational political framework appears the most effective method of recent times by which these unfortunate peoples can realize a form of national autonomy. Hence the Soviet Union has gained sincere partisans among the minorities of Central Asia.

During the wartime occupation of northern Iran, the Soviet Government was able to cultivate a vociferous element of a particularly independent people. The Kurds, of whom there are roughly between three and four million, are a predatory, backward race scattered mainly through five nations but who nevertheless have managed to keep alive their traditions and national identity over a great period of time. The main portion of Kurds, about 1,500,000, live in Turkey; however, the development of Turkish nationalism has left little room for the development of Kurdish nationalism and has in fact worked against it. There are another 800,000 Kurds in Iraq who are said to live an unpersecuted nomadic existence but who have received no encouragement toward progressive cultural or national development. This is generally the condition of the 250,000 Kurds in Syria. In Iran, there are in the vicinity of 500,000 Kurds who, while not greatly persecuted, are not encouraged in their national development. The remaining Kurds, supposedly about 40,000, reside in the Armenian Republic of the Soviet Union.

The dream of Kurdish nationalists is a Kurdish state. As envisioned by them, this state would stretch in an arc from Luristan in the southeast to Malatia in the west, its length being about 600 miles and its maximum width about 200 miles. The proposed Kurdish state would reach approximately from the Mediterranean littoral to that of the Persian Gulf, and cut through the territory of five states with Kurdish populations. Needless to say, control of such a country would be of tremendous strategic importance to any great nation desiring strong influence in the Near East.

The Kurds in the USSR have received particular attention in regard to their cultural autonomy and national development. This, of course, is fully in line with the Soviet multinational policy. In the Kurd districts of Armenia, the Kurdish language has been used in the primary schools, a Kurdish college has been established, a weekly journal in Kurdish has been published, and the study and revival of Kurdish folklore encouraged.[1] This development of Kurdish nationalism within the USSR has stretched in influence all through the Kurdish lands of the Near East.

When Soviet troops occupied Iran in 1941, they came into contact with a portion of the half-million Iranian Kurds. Indications are that Soviet Russia was initially so completely occupied with Germany in the west that she was unable to devote any time toward her Kurdish ambitions. Early in 1942, she nevertheless rounded up a group of Kurdish leaders and took them to Baku for a grand conclave. However, following that short affair, there was no further Soviet activity until the first part of 1944.

In the meantime, apparently without Russian support, a Kurdish nationalist movement developed in the Iranian town of Mahabad. Composed of a number of prominent young Kurds, it was called the Komala, or Committee for Kurdish Youth, and in a relatively short time gained great support among all Kurds in Iran. When word of the organization eventually reached British authorities, they decided on a hands-off policy because their commitments to the Arabs did not permit them to cooperate actively with such an organization. To the Russians, however, the Komala was an ideal instrument for furthering plans of Soviet aggrandizement. In 1944, while Soviet organizers concentrated on Azerbaijan exploitation, they also began to extend a helping hand to the Kurdish nationalists. Communist Kurds, offering material aid and assistance from Russia, infiltrated the Komala.[2]

---

[1] W. G. Elphinston, "The Kurdish Question", *International Affairs*, January 1946, pp. 91-103.

[2] Archie Roosevelt Jr., "The Kurdish Republic of Mahabad," *op. cit.*

By 1945, the Soviet position in northern Iran was strong enough and that of the Iranian Government weak enough so that the Komala could come into the open. In April, Qazi Mohammad, hereditary judge and religious leader of Mahabad, agreed to head a new Kurdish movement for national independence. From the beginning, he relied heavily on the assistance of Soviet advisers. At the same time, a Democratic party of Kurdistan was formed and all Kurdish notables were asked to become members. Many of those asked joined without realizing that their nationalism was being exploited toward Soviet ends.[3]

One of the first acts of the new independence movement was to issue a declaration setting forth Kurdish rights and desires. The declaration called for a large degree of autonomy and self-government and use of the Kurdish language; furthermore, development of educational facilities, natural resources, agricultural lands, health facilities, and commerce, all of which had largely been neglected by the Iranian Government, and all of which might be considered justifiable desires. A good clue as to who originated the document, however, was apparent in the last line of the declaration, which stated: "Long Live Kurdish Democratic Autonomy!!"

In December 1945, when the armed Azerbaijan "Democrats", aided by the Red Army, seized control of Azerbaijan province, the nearby areas of the Kurdish autonomy movement were thus also freed from Iranian Government control. At this point Qazi Mohammad, the Kurd independence leader, and his advisers from the North decided that they could end the fiction of autonomy within the Iranian State and declare their complete independence. Archie Roosevelt Jr., Assistant U. S. Military Attaché in Iran, wrote of this event that "on December 15, 1945, at a meeting in Mahabad attended by tribal chiefs, the leaders of the new Kurdish Democrat party, and three Soviet officers in a jeep, armed with tommy-guns, solemnly inaugurated the Kurdish People's Government and raised the Kurdish flag." Five of the new leaders received the rank of "Marshal" and were "provided with Soviet uniforms, complete with high boots, stiff shoulder-straps, and red-banded garrison caps."[4]

The new Kurdish Republic was hardly as grand as Kurdish nationalists had envisioned, nor did it control more than a few thousand of the four million Kurds. In fact, the area of actual sovereignty included only one town of consequence, Mahabad, and the villages of Bokan, Naqedeh and Ushunuieh. Shortly after its inception, the new

3 Roosevelt, *op. cit.*
4 Roosevelt, *op. cit.*

government became involved in a territorial dispute with the autonomous Azerbaijan People's Government. It seemed that in the territory between the newly created Soviet dependencies was an area of plains and mountains. On the plains lived Azerbaijanis but in the mountains lived Kurdish tribes. The areas were claimed by both regimes and were therefore a source of continuous friction. The Soviets were naturally anxious to settle the dispute in order that autonomous Azerbaijan could present a strong front in negotiating with the Teheran Government over its future autonomous status. Therefore, a treaty was negotiated under Minindel auspices between the so-called Kurdish and Azerbaijan Republics. This treaty aroused great concern in Teheran since it indicated the two Soviet-sponsored regimes within Iranian territory considered themselves independent sovereignties with the right to make treaties and exchange diplomatic envoys. The text of the Kurdish-Azerbaijan Treaty consisted of seven articles which stated:

"1. The two signatory governments will exchange representatives whenever it is deemed advisable.

"2. In those areas of Azerbaijan where there are Kurdish minorities, Kurds will be appointed to government departments, and in those areas where there are Azerbaijan minorities, Azerbaijanis will be appointed to government departments.

"3. A joint economic commission will be formed to solve the economic problems of the signatory nations. Members of this commission will be appointed by the heads of the national governments.

"4. The military forces of the signatory nations will assist each other whenever necessary.

"5. Any negotiations with the Teheran Government will be conducted in the joint interest of the Azerbaijan and Kurdish national governments.

"6. The Azerbaijan National Government will take the necessary steps to promote the use of the Kurdish language and the development of Kurdish culture among the Kurds of Azerbaijan, and the Kurdish National Government will take similar steps with regard to the Azerbaijanis living in Kurdistan.

"7. Both signatory nations will take measures to punish any individual or group seeking to destroy the historic friendship and democratic brotherhood of the Azerbaijanis and Kurds."[5]

This document is noteworthy for more than the fact that it indicates recognition of national sovereignty by the two parties. It is in addition an economic and military pact, but more important still, it

[5] Roosevelt, *op. cit.*

reflects in articles two and six the principles of the Soviet nationality policy and the recognition of minority rights within these Communist satellites. The most interesting aspect of these provisions, however, was their complete failure in actual practice. In this case, as in so many others, it developed that Communists were also nationalists and tended to promote their own interests in advance of either Russian or world Communist interests.

This is illustrated by the subsequent peace settlement between Azerbaijan and Teheran in which all Azerbaijan, including the Kurdish areas, became an autonomous region of Iran. The Kurds understandably reacted bitterly to this arrangement. They had done little more than advance from a minority in Iran to a minority in Azerbaijan. Consequently, Qazi Mohammad travelled to Teheran and negotiated personally with Iranian Premier Ghavam. He asked that his Kurdish areas of Azerbaijan and the Kurdish areas controlled by the Iran Government be formed into an autonomous province within the Iranian nation and that its governor and its army garrison be picked from the local population. Ghavam immediately agreed on one condition (as he had done with the Soviets in regard to the oil question): that Qazi obtain the consent of Javid, the Communist governor of autonomous Azerbaijan. Javid, in spite of the Kurd-Azerbaijan treaty, was not favorably disposed to the partial dismemberment of his already small territory even for the benefit of the "brother Kurds", and indignantly rejected Qazi's proposal. The friction between the two Soviet dependencies therefore continued.

Unfortunately for them, however, as time progressed and the last traces of Red Army control vanished, the strength of the Iranian Government in Teheran became progressively greater. Soviet promises to supply arms for the defense of the Kurdish State were not fulfilled and the burden therefore fell on a few ill-equipped tribes. Thus by autumn of 1946, Iranian Government troops were able to occupy nearly all of the Kurdish Republic, and on December 15, 1946, Government troops entered Mahabad and ended the ill-fated Kurdish State.[6]

In the final analysis then, the Soviet strategy with the Kurds failed in the same ignominious manner that it failed with the Azerbaijanis. USSR aims were revealed, however, and whenever it appears tactically advantageous, the Kurdish independence movement will be pushed once again. The principal advantage of a Soviet-dominated Kurdish nation would be the strong position achieved by the Kremlin in Near

[6] For additional material on the Kurdish State see Roosevelt, *op. cit.;* Elphinston, *op. cit.; Soviet News,* August 28, 1946; *New York Times,* April 4, 6, 1946.

and Middle Eastern affairs—strategically a complete Kurdistan would provide a link between the Mediterranean and the Persian Gulf, the implications of which are strikingly apparent. Moreover, with a nominally independent Kurdistan, the Soviet Union would gain yet another voice in world politics. Such a state is not, however, likely to evolve in its envisioned entirety, at least under USSR auspices. If it should originate it would be under British tutorship, for in the foreseeable future British influence will probably continue to predominate in the areas of the proposed Kurdish state. Since the British seem unlikely to effect a change in the existing structure, there appears little likelihood of a united Kurdistan for some time to come.

To summarize, Soviet Russia attempted to exploit a temporary internal political problem of Iran into a Communist territorial acquisition, but was unsuccessful. Soviet methods, however, were not without effect and can be considered good enough for use in almost any section of Asia at any time in the near future. As long as the USSR can offer a few material benefits and promote cultural, educational, and material development for the forgotten races in Asia, its program of aggrandizement will always have an excellent chance of success.

Afghanistan

From a Soviet viewpoint, Afghanistan is a target similar to Iran. Lying almost in the center of Asia, this country was once a great crossroad for trade and travel between the Near East and India, and during the nineteenth century it was also an area of constant conflict between Russia and Britain.[7] Today, it comprises a population of between nine and ten million most of whom are herdsmen or small farmers. Nearly a quarter of this population is nomadic.

According to the Soviet viewpoint,[8] Afghanistan is ethnologically an imperfect nation. The country was created as a buffer state against Tsarist Russian expansion by Britain, claimed the Soviets, and little consideration was given to the different races making up the population. Moreover, the country's borders contained districts in the north

[7] Early in 1873, the British succeeded in obtaining from the Russians a declaration that Afghanistan was beyond the sphere of Russian influence. But by 1879, Russian intrigue forced the British temporarily out of the country. They returned, however, in force and compelled the Afghans to accept a British resident, and to subordinate foreign affairs to British influence. By an Anglo-Russian Convention in 1907, Russia recognized British predominance in the area. In 1919, after a short conflict with the British, Afghanistan gained the right to carry on her own foreign relations. British influence nevertheless continued to remain strong.

[8] New Times, Moscow, April 1, 1946, article by M. Malakhov, "Afghanistan."

populated by Turkmens, Uzbeks, and Tajiks; in the south, on the other hand, over four million (4,178,500) Afghans—native stock—were cut off from their country and joined to India and to Baluchistan. According to Soviet figures, the chief nationalities inhabiting Afghanistan are the Afghans (4,484,562), Tajiks (2,106,000), Uzbeks (802,000), and the Hazara (867,000). The remainder of the population is made up of Turkmens, Nursitans, Taimani, Firuzkuhs, Jamshidis, Taimuris, Baluchi, Arabs, Indians, Turkic tribes, Jews, Kiani, Kurds, and Kipchaks. In the south, the Soviets agreed that the population is made up of Afghan tribes, but in the rest of the country or the section lying north of the Hindu Kush, they maintained that Afghans constitute an insignificant minority.[9]

As with other nations bordering the USSR, the Minindel considered that a border adjustment with Afghanistan was necessary following World War II. For a change, however, this "adjustment" did not work out to the particular disadvantage of the bordering state. Or, as the Soviets said, "The agreement exemplifies once again the attentive attitude of the Soviet Government towards the rights and needs of small nations, and will undoubtedly help forward the further development and consolidation of friendly relations between the Soviet Union and Afghanistan."[10] For the most part, the boundary adjustment signed June 13, 1946, merely reaffirmed and clarified the existing boundary along the center of the navigable and nonnavigable parts of the Amu-Darya (Oxus) river and the Panja river. The agreement also provided for the re-demarcation of the frontier signs on the land sectors of the Soviet-Afghan boundary, or between the Turkmen Soviet Republic and Afghanistan. The destruction of many of these signs had led at times to undesirable frontier disputes. Further, the agreement provided for the utilization of certain water rights on the Kushka River and the erection of a Soviet dam on the Murgab River in the Turkmen frontier sector. And lastly, the two nations agreed to render invalid Articles 9 and 10 of the Soviet-Afghan Treaty of February 28, 1921. These articles concerned the incorporation into Afghanistan of the Kushka district, should it be so desired by the local population, and the rendering of Soviet financial and material aid to Afghanistan.[11] The Afghans had never made any great effort to affix the Kushka district to their country, and the territory had remained a part of Soviet Turkmenia. Judging from other Soviet-conducted plebiscites that have sampled the will of

[9] *New Times*, April 1, 1946.
[10] *Soviet News*, June 15, 1946.
[11] *Ibid.*

the people, it is extremely doubtful if the population would have expressed a desire to unite with Afghanistan. However, the new arrangement invalidated any future claim by Afghanistan to the Kushka area.

The only place where the Afghan-Soviet border remained somewhat indefinite was in the eastern panhandle where Afghanistan touches Chinese Sinkiang, and where India is but a matter of miles from the USSR. Actually the demarcation of international boundaries at this meeting point was of little concern to any of the four powers, in that the area is one of the most desolate, rugged, and inaccessible places on earth. The only method of transportation through this territory is the 20,740 foot Kilik Pass and the chances are that it will never be too heavily traveled.

Of greatest concern to Afghanistan were the sizable minorities of Uzbeks and Tajiks, both of whom had Soviet Republics bordering on Afghanistan to the north. In actual fact, Afghanistan contains nearly 1,000,000 more Tajiks than the Tajik Soviet Republic, but as far as Soviet policy is concerned the Soviet Tajik Republic is the legitimate representative of all Tajik interests, cultural and otherwise. Although one out of every five people in Afghanistan is a Tajik (ethnically similar to the Iranians), the Soviet Government doubtless looks forward to the day when the Tajik brothers in Afghanistan will be liberated and reunited with the Soviet Tajik nation.

The Soviets have done a great deal toward the development of a thriving border city, Stalinabad. This city is located near enough to the Afghan border so that its new buildings, paved streets, its theatre and library, and its Soviet-stimulated, flourishing Tajik culture and industry are presumably irresistible to the Afghanistan Tajiks, who possess no improvements such as these. Stalinabad is located close enough to the border so that some day breathing space might be needed to the south as has been the case with Leningrad and the Karelian Isthmus, and Odessa with Bessarabia. The Soviet Tajiks, like all other Soviet Asians, exhibit material benefits to their kindred peoples on the other side of the border, thus paving the way for any future aggrandizement.

To a slightly lesser degree the Uzbek minority of Afghanistan faces problems like those confronting the Tajiks. Uzbek development and culture in the Soviet Union might well prove just as irresistible to the 800,000 Afghan Uzbeks as Soviet Tajik culture and other benefits are intended to be the Afghan Tajiks.

There are other great attractions in Afghanistan for the Soviet Union. The nationality conglomeration can merely be used as a means toward these more important ends. One of these ends is oil. According to Soviet scientists, oil deposits exist in northwestern Afghanistan. The USSR would doubtless be very interested in developing these for its own markets. More important than the oil, however, is the fact that Afghanistan is the continental gateway to India. Properly developed, Soviet strategy can be used to excellent advantage on millions and millions of Indians. On the sub-continent live a large section of the earth's population, which is perhaps too large and too stable to be affected by the alien philosophy of Karl Marx, but which is nevertheless a potential field for Communist development. Afghanistan is the passageway to India and there is no visible deterring factor if Soviet Russia desires to use it.

CHAPTER 15

CONFIRMATIONS AND ASPIRATIONS

"We do not want a single bit of foreign land, but at the same time not an inch of our land shall ever be yielded to anyone else."—Stalin, Sixteenth Congress, Communist Party Soviet Union.

Armistice agreements, peace treaties, and postwar conferences and settlements confirmed earlier Soviet territorial acquisitions, realized additional territory for the USSR, and revealed still further ambitions of the Kremlin policy makers.

Finland, it will be recalled, waged an unexpected 104-day war with the Soviet Union in 1939-40 and as a result was forced to cede great amounts of her territory to the land-hungry USSR. Later, anxious for revenge, Finland became allied with Nazi Germany, and when that nation attacked the USSR, Finland soon found herself again at war with Russia. With German assistance the Finns initially not only regained what had been lost in 1940, but much of Karelia in addition. However, even though the Finns expressed the desire to get out of the war with their regained territories, it was impossible as long as they were allied with Germany. And Germany was in no position to allow the Finns to withdraw as long as the Finnish area was of strategic value to her. Nevertheless, Finland attempted to negotiate peace with the Soviet Union in February 1944 on the basis of the restoration of the 1939 frontiers. The Soviets replied that Finland could have peace by agreeing to break off relations with Germany, intern German troops and ships, release prisoners of war, restore the 1940 frontier, and continue negotiations regarding demobilization plans, reparations, and the status of Petsamo.

This solution was unacceptable to the Finns. Armistice negotiations continued, but by April 1944 they had reached an impasse and were broken off. Shortly thereafter, in June, the Red Army launched a big offensive and succeeded in recapturing Viborg and part of the Karelian Isthmus. By this time the war was going badly for the Axis. Germany was exerting strong pressure on all of her satellites and especially on the Finns to stay in the war, but by August the situation had become so hopeless that the Finns were compelled to ask for an armistice at Soviet terms. Although German troops continued to occupy large sections of the country until they were driven out at the end of the year, an armistice was signed on September 19, 1944.

The armistice was actually in the form of a peace treaty between the USSR and Finland although it was negotiated on behalf of the Allied Powers at war with Finland. Its territorial provisions were subsequently confirmed when the final treaty was signed in Paris on February 10, 1947. The terms confirmed the Soviet acquisitions of 1940, and in addition provided for the cession of even more territory to the USSR. The biggest losses to Finland were 5,147.5 square miles of Petsamo area in the extreme north, whereby the Soviet Union gained valuable nickel deposits, nickel mines, and an area with considerable potential mineral deposits. Further, the new land established a greater area of defense in depth for nearby Murmansk. The ceded territory also cut off the Finns from access to the Barents Sea, and at the same time established for the USSR a new common border with Norway in the north. This desire for common borders as a means of influence and control, it will be recalled, has been a strong motive of postwar Soviet policy. Even though the Norwegian border is desolate and in the Arctic Circle, it at least provides a greater degree of influence in Norway than Russia previously exerted.

The second acquisition was 237.5 square miles of the Porkkala area, leased for use as a Red Fleet naval base for a period of fifty years. This leasehold gave the Soviet Union even stronger defenses against possible sea attack through the Gulf of Finland. It also placed still more Soviet armed forces on Finnish soil in addition to those already stationed on the Hanko Lease. Under such circumstances, it was extremely unlikely that Finland would be in a position to pursue any policy not in accord with Soviet policy.

In addition to these acquisitions, it was reported on February 3, 1947, that Finland had been compelled to cede 110 square miles of territory adjoining the Petsamo area. This territory was ceded under the Soviet-Finnish agreement covering ex-German assets in Finland.[1] Still later (on July 15, 1947), Finland transferred, under the same agreement, 67.5 square miles of the Paatsjoki region.[2] Thus, in the final analysis, the USSR acquired better than 19,000 square miles from Fin-

[1] *New York Times*, February 18, 1947.
[2] *Ibid.*, July 17, 1947.

land during an eight year period between 1939 and 1947.[3] Presumably this was enough to satisfy all Soviet territorial desires in this area. The only thing that remained was the replacement of the government in power by one completely subservient to USSR desires. This change can perhaps be engineered at almost any time the Soviet Union considers it necessary.

With Rumania, an armistice was signed September 12, 1944 just one week prior to the Finnish armistice. The terms confirmed the 1940 cession of Bessarabia and Northern Bucovina to the USSR. This decision was reaffirmed in the final peace treaty signed February 10, 1947 in Paris, and thereby the seizure of 19,446 square miles of Rumanian territory and 3,700,000 people was approved by both the United States and Great Britain. The naked postwar display of force and threats by the USSR, direct interference anad intervention by Vyshinsky, and the subsequent overthrow of the Rumanian Government in February 1945 were therefore also sanctioned, perhaps reluctantly, by those nations signatory to the Rumanian Peace Treaty. It should not soon be forgotten that Vyshinski told the Rumanian King that unless a government were installed according to Soviet specifications it would be considered a hostile act against the Soviet Union. "I will not otherwise be able to guarantee the independence of Rumania," said Vyshinski.[4] As it worked out in the end, it was six of one and half a dozen of another.

That Soviet Russia's territorial aims extended considerably beyond her immediate border areas was revealed on the opening day of the Potsdam conference in July 1945. To a rather startled Truman and Churchill, Stalin indicated his desire to discuss trusteeships. He stated bluntly that the Soviet Union "would like some territory of the defeated states."[5] The Russian delegation accordingly presented a memorandum proposing that the USSR be named trustee of one of the Italian colonies, preferably Tripolitania. However, due to the immediate and perhaps understandable recalcitrance of Mr. Churchill, the matter was set aside for future discussion by the Foreign Ministers.

---

[3] Territorial acquisitions from Finland were as follows (square miles):

Karelian Isthmus, Lake Ladoga.	10,570.19	Petsamo area	5,147.5
Four Islands, Gulf of Finland.	19.07	Porkkala-Udd (Lease)	237.5
"Salla" Sector	3,010.33	Territory ceded February 3, 1947	110.
Fishermans Peninsula	143.9	Territory ceded July 15, 1947..	67.5
Hanko (Lease)	45.18		
		GRAND TOTAL	19,351.17

[4] Paul Winterton, "The Aims of the USSR in Europe," *International Affairs,* January 1946, pp. 14-27.

[5] Byrnes, *op. cit.,* p. 76.

At the September 1945 London Foreign Minister's Conference, the USSR accordingly advanced once again the trusteeship ideas expressed at Potsdam. The Soviet delegation, said Molotov, proposed that the principle of trusteeship be applied to the Italian colonies with individual nations acting as trustee for each of these colonies. The Soviet Union desired one of these trusteeships. The USSR, he continued, had had wide experience "establishing friendly relations between different nationalities," and such experience could naturally be applied to the administration of Tripolitania. Ten years, Molotov believed, would be adequate to prepare the territory for its independent existence. The basic reasons for Soviet control were that the Soviet Union had a sea outlet in the north, and in view of its vast territory should have one in the south, "especially", said Molotov, "since we now have the right to use Dairen and Port Arthur in the Far East." Furthermore, "the Soviet Union should take the place that is due it, and should have bases in the Mediterranean for its merchant fleet." Molotov concluded: "We do not propose to introduce the Soviet system into this territory apart from the democratic order that is desired by the people. . . This will not be done along the lines that have been used in Greece."[6] The last statement, of course, could hardly have promoted much enthusiasm on the part of the British for professed Soviet desires.

At the same time, the Soviets evidenced a very lively interest in the disposition of the Dodecanese Islands. Four of the five Foreign Ministers believed that the strategically located islands should be restored to Greece. The fifth, Mr. Molotov, did not. The decision on these islands could be made only in connection with a decision on the Italian colonies, he maintained.

The Soviet position did not change appreciably either on the Dodecanese or on Tripolitania until January 1946. Molotov then advanced a proposal for two-power trusteeships whereby Italy and one other power would administer each territory jointly. In regard to Tripolitania, suggested Molotov, the other power should be the Soviet Union. The proposal, however, was completely unacceptable to the British who by this time were determined to keep the USSR out of the Mediterranean in any guise or form.

The Soviet position in regard to the Dodecanese remained unchanged until June 1946, when Molotov abruptly agreed that the Dodecanese should go to Greece, and that in accordance with an American proposal a decision on the Italian colonies be postponed a year, after which, if no agreement were reached, the United Nations General

6 Byrnes, *op. cit.*, pp. 94-6.

Assembly would be asked for a decision. From this time on, the Russians' attitude appears to have evolved to a point where by 1948 they favored Italian trusteeship for the former Italian colonies. At the same time, Soviet spokesmen have continued to maintain that in regard to territorial administration the USSR is "the greatest progressive force in the international arena."[7]

The Soviet Union also expressed interest in another section of the Mediterranean—Tangier. When the Western Powers decided to call a conference to settle the future of the international zone in June 1945, Soviet Russia protested, maintaining that she was entitled to be represented and that she had not been asked. The Soviet contention was based on the grounds that Tsarist Russia had been a party to the Treaty of Algeciras in 1906 which had recognized the international character of the zone and established a governing regime.[8] Soviet Russia had not, however, been a party to the 1923 Statute of Tangier which revised the earlier treaty, but for that matter neither had the United States. For this reason, the June conference was called off.

At Potsdam it was decided that the Tangier Zone should remain internationalized and that its new status would be discussed the following month in Paris by France, the U.S., Britain, and the USSR.

The Paris conference which followed agreed that a provisional international administration would be established composed of the four powers and Spain. The USSR objected to Spain's inclusion but was assured that a conference would be held the following year at which time Spain would be excluded if Franco were still in power. Other features of the Zone's administration were to continue as they had in the past until such a time as a new Statute was decided upon.

Interestingly enough, after insisting upon the right to participate and being included in the provisional administration, the Soviet Union took no further action on the matter. The Zone continued to function generally as it had before the war. Nevertheless, the Soviet Government had asserted itself and laid claim to joint-administration of the entrance port to the Mediterranean. If it so desired, therefore, the USSR could use the International Zone of Tangier as headquarters in North Africa and as a place from which to assert some influence as a Mediterranean power. In addition, if interested in the economic advantages to be derived from the area, the USSR could make use of the port facilities and the free trade zone. These were Soviet prerogatives and they could and would be used at the discretion of Soviet authorities.

[7] Radio Moscow, December 24, 1948; *New York Times,* December 25, 1948.

[8] Yet another example of an interesting Soviet tactic—attempting to gather in all the benefits of the Tsar while generally evading the obligations of the Tsar.

The reasoning underlying Soviet aspirations for Tripolitania was more complex. With a base in Africa, Soviet Russia would be more clearly justified in demanding greater control of the Straits. At the same time, with territory in the Mediterranean, the USSR could greatly increase its voice in Mediterranean and world naval affairs. Tripolitania had been a costly expenditure for the Italians, but to the Soviet Union it could doubtless prove a fine base for the dissemination of Communist ideas in North Africa. Strategically, Tripolitania would have enabled the USSR to equalize Western defense bases in the Mediterranean. Britain, of course, regarded the Soviet claim to the Italian colony as a direct threat to her line with the Far East and as an unhealthy influence in the affairs of the Near and Middle East. She was therefore determined to keep the Russians out of the Mediterranean at any cost, notwithstanding the *Pravda* contention that "not a single geography book says the Mediterranean is a British sea nor its colonies British territory."[9]

As to the Dodecanese, although the USSR advanced no known claims on these islands the Russians nevertheless withheld settlement of the Dodecanese question pending a solution favorable to their aims in Tripolitania. They apparently desired to use the islands as a bargaining point, or possibly as military bases to control the entrance to the Straits. Whatever the case, the Soviets finally agreed to settle the issue with the same surprising alacrity with which they agreed to drop their claim for Tripolitania. Thus the Soviet Union, as suddenly as it had asserted its intentions in the Mediterranean in 1945, just as suddenly dropped them in 1946. Even in Tangier, where they received a voice in the administration and control of the Zone, the Russians withdrew quietly after their initial declaration of intent.

Thus Soviet territorial ambitions had been revealed, but little had been accomplished towards their realization. It was perhaps an indication that USSR expansion would continue to be primarily from the central land mass of the Soviet Union and not beyond this point of centralized control. Nevertheless, reports from widely different areas in the world indicated that the USSR was at least interested in territorial acquisitions beyond its immediate borders. It should be noted that such reports have often preindicated Soviet territorial aspirations, and have often been verified by subsequent events.

Even in the Americas there have been scattered reports of Russian territorial desires. It was reported on October 28, 1946, in Lima, Peru, for instance, that Russian representatives had made efforts to obtain

9 *Pravda*, September 23, 1945.

fishing rights from Ecuador in the Galapagos Islands. The waters around these islands are admittedly one of the best tuna fishing areas in the world, but the islands themselves are doubtless more important as a key defense point of the Panama Canal. The report was of course denied by both Ecuador and the USSR.[10]

Other unconfirmed reports, usually denied by both parties, maintained that the Soviet Union was seeking bases in two widely separate areas: a traffic harbor at Seydisfjord on the east coast of Iceland[11] and Formosa off the coast of China.[12] Farther to the north, there were reports of Soviet interest in Alaska. During 1948 Russian radio propaganda announced that the U.S. claim to Alaska was void and had ceased to be valid as of December 1947. The Soviet contention was thus presumably based on a theory that this territory had been sold in 1867 for a period of only eighty years, although there was no clause in the transfer agreement to this effect. Moreover, the Soviets contended that Alaska's transfer to the U.S. for $7,200,000 was a wrongful act of the Tsarist Government and consequently could be considered invalid. The USSR also advanced similar but less frequent claims to California on the basis of Russian exploration and settlement during the late eighteenth and early nineteenth century.[13]

In addition, the USSR demonstrated considerable interest in the Polar regions. Soviet claims in the north related to exploration and discovery of the ice cap, but did not pertain to any of the non-Russian Arctic land masses. In regard to the ice-covered continent of Antarctica, however, the Soviet Government evidenced considerable concern. Russian claims to this region were based primarily on the famous Bellingshausen-Lazarev expedition of 1819 which sighted and claimed the first land inside the Antarctic circle. The Soviet claim, however, was modest and did not extend to the whole continent. It merely asserted the Soviet right of participation in any international settlement of Antarctic questions along with Britain, New Zealand, Australia, France, the U.S., Norway, Argentina, and Chile.[14]

Still other unconfirmed reports discussed Soviet intentions in Europe. For instance, it was reported in September 1946 that Albania had secretly granted rights to the USSR on Saseno Island upon which the Soviet Union planned to build a large air and naval base. Tass, the

10 *New York Times,* October 29, November 1, 5, 18, 1946.
11 *Ibid.,* May 22, 1948.
12 *Ibid.,* January 30, 1946.
13 *Ibid.,* May 11, 1945.
14 *Izvestiya, Pravda,* February 11, 1949; *New York Times,* February 12, 1949.

Soviet news agency, denied the report and attributed it to sources anxious "to justify and cover up provocative actions of Greek Royalist Fascists on the Albanian frontier."[15]

Again, reports preindicating the establishment of an East German People's Democracy began to appear shortly after the Western Powers instigated plans for a bi- and tri-zonal Germany.

More interesting were reports regarding the future incorporation of Rumania and Bulgaria into the USSR. They began to appear during the early summer of 1948. The Kremlin supposedly exerted considerable pressure at this time to have the Rumanians conduct a plebiscite by which the people would express their overwhelming desire to become a Soviet Republic within the USSR. After the Rumanian plebiscite, Bulgaria would similarly express a spontaneous desire to become a member of the Soviet Union. The Soviets would thus gain a common border with Greece and European Turkey and would realize an historic aspiration of Russian foreign policy. Reports of this plan of incorporation were said to have been carefully checked and confirmed.[16] The organ of the Cominform in Bucharest, moreover, did not deny these May reports until the following September.[17]

There is reason to believe that such action on the part of the USSR was certainly not beyond the realm of possibility. However, there were equally good reasons why the reports might be considered premature. For all actual purposes the two regimes were at that moment almost as much under the influence of the USSR as was Soviet Estonia. As long as they maintained the fiction of independence and continued to operate as legally constituted states, they could express the ideas and forward the program of the Soviet Union more effectively than if they were Soviet Socialist Republics. Not until the time when they no longer served the interests of the USSR as independent states, would they express their inspired desire to join the Soviet Union.

In the final analysis, these combined reports add credulity to the assumption that Soviet territorial aspirations know no bounds. The territories already seized have apparently been but the detonator of still grander aims.

15 New York Times, September 17, 1946.
16 Ibid., May 10-30, 1948.
17 For a Lasting Peace, For a People's Democracy, Bucharest, September 1, 1948.

CHAPTER 16

CONCEPTS AND METHODS

"We know that time is on our side, and that it works for us."—Ilya Ehrenburg, "Soviet Weekly," May 6, 1948.

Among the basic concepts of Soviet expansion is Communist theory itself. To illustrate Communist theory as it applies to expansion, one must first turn to the interpretations of Marxism-Leninism by the Communist Party's primary theoretician, Joseph Stalin, who has clearly reiterated and elaborated the Communist assumption that revolution is a necessity in the change from capitalism to socialism. This idea was inherent in earliest Communist doctrine long before the twentieth century. In the *Communist Manifesto,* for instance, written more than one hundred years ago, the concept of revolution, world revolution, was stressed by Marx and Engels. The thought was later expanded by Marx in the study *Capital* and developed still further by Lenin. In interpretations of these original theories, Stalin states that, "revolutionary overturns produced by oppressed classes are a perfectly natural and inevitable phenomenon. The transition from capitalism to socialism can be accomplished not by means of slow change, not by means of reform, but only by means of qualitative change of the capitalist system, by means of revolution."[1] This revolution, says Stalin, is the world revolution of the proletariat. "The epoch of world revolution", he continues, began in 1917. It was instigated and will continue only through conscious human effort, and once begun must be fought to a finish.[2]

The goal of this revolution, according to Stalin, "is to consolidate the dictatorship of the proletariat in one country, using it as a base for

[1] *History of the All-Union Communist Party* (Moscow, 1938), pp. 101-5. (*Istoriia Vsesoiuznoi Kommunisticheskoi Partii,* Moskva, 1938-1946.)

[2] Stalin, *Problems of Leninism* (Moscow, 1945), p. 54. (*Voprosy Leninizma,* Moskva, 1945, eleventh edition). And "Historicus", "Stalin on Revolution", *Foreign Affairs,* January 1949.

the overthrow of imperialism in all countries."[3] Imperialism by Soviet interpretation implies exploitation through capitalism. But Stalin elaborates further on the consolidation of the proletarian dictatorship. "The development of world revolution," he says, "will be more rapid and more thorough, the more thoroughly Socialism fortifies itself in the first victorious country, [and] the faster this country is transformed into a base for the further unfolding of world revolution, [or] into a lever for the further disintegration of imperialism. . . . The development of world revolution will be the more rapid and thorough, the more effective the aid rendered by the first Socialist country to the workers . . . of all other countries." This aid should be expressed first, says Stalin, by "carrying out the maximum realizable in one country for the development, support, awakening of revolution in all countries;" and second by the victorious proletariat in this one country standing up "against the remaining capitalist world, attracting to itself the oppressed classes of other countries, raising revolts in those countries against the capitalists, [and] in the event of necessity, coming out even with armed force against the exploiting classes and their governments."[4]

It is interesting to note in this relation that the 1938 Communist Party History carries on its title page the slogan "Workers of all countries, unit!"[5] This history states in its introduction: "Studying the history of the Communist Party Soviet Union strengthens confidence in the final victory of the great cause of the party of Lenin and Stalin, the victory of Communism in the whole world." To this can be added the belief of Lenin that "the victory of proletarian revolutions in

[3] Stalin, *Problems, op. cit.*, p. 54. In relation to the above subject Professor Paul Mantoux, Director of the Graduate Institute of International Studies in Geneva, Switzerland, made two keen observations which the author feels should be included. First, that it should be remembered that Stalin is not an original thinker in the sense that are Marx, Engels, and Lenin (a disciple of the former two). "The importance of his writings or utterances lies in their relation to his actions," says Mantoux. Secondly, that "it is very probable that Lenin, when he started his revolution, considered it essentially as the beginning of the world revolution—the fact that it happened to begin in Russia being merely incidental. Being a Russian by birth and knowing the conditions which in 1917 made the success of his enterprise in Russia possible, he did there what he could certainly not have succeeded in doing in any other great country. But it is very likely that in his mind Russia and the welfare of the Russian people, were only a means to a much greater aim, or to say the least the first step towards a universal goal."

[4] *Ibid.*, p. 104.

[5] Repeating the famous slogan in Marx and Engels' *Communist Manifesto* of 1848, and now echoed daily in the Communist Party organs *Pravda* and *Izvestiya*.

capitalist countries is a vital interest of the toilers of the USSR."[6]

Certainly the implication of these thoughts is that the socialist motherland, the USSR, is theoretically expansionist and would therefore sanction extension of its borders in that it is thus freeing more territory from capitalist exploitation or imperialism. Its acts since 1939 would confirm that it is authentically expansionist as well. What is more, this expansionism is a fervent missionary crusade aimed at liberating the world proletariat from bourgeois enslavement. Stalin, in a pledge to the Soviet saviour, Lenin, says, "We swear to thee, Comrade Lenin, that we will not spare our life in order to strengthen and expand the union of toilers of the whole world."[7]

But this expansionism is not called expansionism in Communist theory. It is instead termed the liberation of lands and toilers from capitalist exploitation. It is a tenet of Marxism-Leninism in that it furthers the aim of a world union of socialist states and peoples. It was as much a righteous and justifiable act to the Communist prophet Lenin as it is now to his disciple Stalin.

Nor, similarly, is aggression actually considered aggression. N. Rubinstein, an official Communist theoretician, says that the Bolsheviks "recognized the justice of wars of liberation, non-aggressive wars, the aim of which is to defend a nation against outside attack and attempts to enslave it, or to deliver the people from capitalist servitude, or, lastly, to liberate a colony or dependent country from oppression by the imperialists."[8] This reasoning can be used to justify every contemplated, attempted, or realized Soviet act of aggression and aggrandizement since 1939. And for that matter any comparable act any time, anywhere.

Furthermore, Rubinstein's interpretations as well as Stalin's expound the role to be played by the Red Army. In addition to its task of defending the socialist motherland against capitalist encirclement, it is also an implement for the emancipation of the toiling masses in justifiable wars of liberation. In this regard, one may recall the statement of Marshal Bulganin: "Our armed forces, closely rallied around the Soviet Government, are a reliable bastion of the Soviet Union's foreign policy."[9] Actually, in fact, it is the most reliable bastion of Soviet foreign policy and expansionism. It was important enough so

[6] "Historicus", *op. cit.*, p. 199-200.

[7] Stalin, *History*, *op. cit.*, p. 257.

[8] N. Rubinstein, "Soviet Foreign Policy and its Principles," *New Times*, Moscow, March 17, 1948.

[9] *Soviet Weekly*, March 4, 1948.

that Hitler was forced to place a large section of Europe in the Soviet sphere of influence. It was strong enough to influence the partition of Poland, to incorporate the Baltic States into the Soviet Union, to dismember sections of Finland, to acquire Northern Bucovina and Bessarabia. It was powerful enough to promote the establishment of "People's Democracies" in Eastern Europe. It was of such value that Roosevelt and Churchill sacrificed a portion of Europe and consented to the dismemberment of allied China. All other techniques, theories, and methods have been important, but it must be admitted that they have also been ineffective without "that reliable bastion of Soviet foreign policy", the Red Army.

Historically, however, Russia had a long history of expansion and aggrandizement before it became the socialist motherland. These historic trends were strikingly evident in the 1939-1949 period of expansion.

Poland, for instance, has been an object of Russia's eastern expansion for hundreds of years. Tsarist Russia took a leading part in the three partitions of 1772, 1792, and 1795. The partition of Poland by Soviet Russia in 1939 was merely repetition. Even the same ostensible reason used by Catherine in 1772 was advanced by Stalin in 1939: Poland was in a state of anarchy and had ceased to exist.

The search for an outlet on the Baltic Sea is another historic Russian drive. "A window to Europe" on the Baltic was an aim of Peter the Great, who finally realized his ambition after several years of fighting against the armies of Charles XII of Sweden. From then on until the Bolshevik revolution in 1917, the Baltic Coast was at least nominally under the control of Russia. During the two decades of independence enjoyed by Estonia, Latvia, and Lithuania (a part of Poland since the sixteenth century) the Soviet Union gave every outward indication of respecting the sovereignty and independence of these states. However, the alliance with Hitler indicated that Soviet desires for "a window on the Baltic" were as strong as those of Peter. Although Britain and the U.S. refused to recognize the Soviet seizures, the short-lived Baltic republics, excluding Finland, were in 1948 as much or more a part of Soviet Russia as they had been from Peter to Brest-Litovsk.

To the south, Turkey is an historic antagonist of Russia. Catherine both plotted and waged war for control of the Black Sea and seizure of Constantinople and the Straits. She succeeded in the former objective but failed in the latter even after the Russian Navy defeated the Turks in the Black Sea. Nor did subsequent wars alter the situation greatly. However, by the nineteenth century, the decay of the Ottoman Empire had continued to a point where the continuance of Turkey as an independent state rested primarily upon the tangled interests of Russia, France, and Britain. In 1833, the Sultan was forced to agree that during a war the Straits would be available to Russia alone, but this Russian predominance existed only briefly. The Treaty of Paris in 1856 dealt Russian ambitions a crippling blow by neutralizing the Black Sea and Black Sea shores. Even a Russian victory over Turkey in 1877 failed to establish Russia in the desired pre-eminent position, although she did gain Kars and Ardahan as satisfaction for a Turkish war indemnity. For her part in World War I, Russia had planned to acquire control of the Straits and Constantinople, but revolution ended these plans. After the war, the Bolsheviks professed warm friendship for the Turks, but their rapacious instincts were revealed in the 1940 proposed Four Power Pact. These instincts were again laid bare by the presumptuous demands of 1945 and 1946, which at least equalled the most ambitious designs of the Tsars.

Toward Persia, historical Russian aims began with Peter the Great; however, desires for the warm waters of the Persian Gulf did not find expression until the latter part of the nineteenth century. During this period, they launched a conflict with British interests which eventually necessitated the Convention of 1907 whereby Russia and Britain divided Persia into three zones: the south to Britain, the north to Russia, and the middle as a buffer between the two powers. Although the Bolsheviks denounced this agreement, they nevertheless concluded a treaty with Iran in 1921 establishing Soviet Russia as the predominent foreign power in the northern regions once more. The traditional conflict with Britain again came to the forefront when the USSR attempted to seize the northern bordering province of Azerbaijan, exploit Kurdish nationalism, and level vicious propaganda against British imperialism. Soviet territorial ambitions have been directed unrelentingly toward the South. These aims were revealed beyond all shadow of a doubt in the proposed Four Power Pact which stated: ". . . the area in the general direction of the Persian Gulf is recognized as the center of the aspirations of the Soviet Union." The Soviet drive towards the Gulf has been but an intensified continuation of the Tsarist drives in that direction.

Afghanistan, to the east of Persia, is a state which owes its existence to its position as a buffer between Russia and British India. Today India is no longer British and Afghanistan is not much of a buffer.

In the Far East, Russia evidenced interest in Chinese Turkestan or Sinkiang during the latter half of the nineteenth century and this attention has continued in varying degrees until the present. Soviet interest in Mongolia has been characterized by gradual Tsarist and accelerated Communist penetration. In Manchuria and China, the Russian interest dates from before the Treaty of Nerchinsk in 1689. This treaty, the first between a European power and China, caused the Russians to withdraw from colonization south of the Amur River. But the Russian drive resumed at the end of the eighteenth century and continued through the nineteenth century. By the time of the Russo-Japanese War in 1904, Russian influence in Manchuria was preeminent and Tsarist ambitions extended to the south of China. Although the Treaty of Portsmouth replaced Russian domination in the north with Japanese predominance, the Bolsheviks nevertheless attempted to exploit Chinese nationalism in the south following World War I. That Soviet ambitions are equally as strong as those of the Tsars was revealed at Yalta by the expansionist Stalin. To assist in the realization of the historic Russian drive, the Minindel all but openly aided the Chinese Communists in their conquest of China. In actual fact, this historic drive for power in the Far East gives indications of placing the Soviet Union in a far more advantageous position than any other of its territorial drives.

In nearly all of its territorial acquisitions, the Soviet Union has justified its aggrandizement on the basis of historic claims. But these are always difficult to accept as a justification for aggrandizement. The righteousness of irredentism depends on the will of the people, and in this age of international organizations there are free and just ways by which the will of the people can be expressed. The argument that these aggrandized lands once belonged to the Russian Tsars is particularly weak. It is neither more nor less valid than would be a Spanish claim to the Low Countries on the ground that they once belonged to Philip II; a French claim to Mexico because Maximilian reigned briefly behind a carapace of French bayonets; or a German claim to Milwaukee, Wisconsin, on the grounds that the population is of primarily German descent.

The historic drives of Tsarist Russia have been improved by Soviet experience and technique and enlarged by Communist theory. In the concept of territorial expansion, Russianism and Communism are therefore one and the same. The two are synonomous as long as Russia remains the homeland of Marxism-Leninism.

A professed aim of the Soviet Union has been security, and it has used this objective as one of its justifications for expansion. In this connection, the territorial border areas of the USSR must be analyzed as to their defensive and offensive characteristics. For instance, the northern regions of the Arctic constitute a nearly impregnable barrier against attack by land and sea, but are vitally important in considerations of aerial offense or defense. This was the reason why the Soviets demanded bases on icy Spitsbergen. This land is among the most important in the world in an age of inter-continental aerial warfare. Strategically the USSR already possesses nearly half the circumference of the Arctic Circle. The remaining areas are controlled primarily by two great powers, the U.S. and Canada, and one small power, Denmark. Another small nation, Iceland, borders the Circle, and the northern portions of Norway, Sweden, and Finland are within the Arctic area. There is little possibility that Soviet security demands for additional land areas in the Arctic will be made on the U.S. and Canada, but there remains the possibility that future demands will be made on Norway, Iceland, and Denmark. Finland is in a poor position to refuse future territorial demands by the Soviet Union, and Sweden's Arctic areas are outflanked by those of both the Finns and the Norwegians.

On the western frontier, the USSR is protected either by geographic barriers or Kremlin-created buffers. Finland in the north is for all practical purposes a Russian buffer, but in addition the frontier areas are composed of lakes and rivers and, for at least part of the year, the defense is further fortified by the extreme cold. Along the Baltic Sea, the USSR has created Soviet Republics of the formerly independent states of Estonia, Latvia, and Lithuania and thus prevented the possibility of their being used as a beachhead for attack against the land of collectivism. South of Lithuania, the USSR incorporated the former German area of East Prussia[10] and extended the territory of its Polish satellite as far as the port of Stettin, Germany. Thus the Soviets gained control of the eastern and southern shores of the Baltic and went a long way towards making this body of water a Soviet Sea. Moreover, the Kremlin's search for Baltic security apparently extended to the Danish island of Bornholm at the mouth of the Baltic, but because of international pressure and political considerations in Scandinavia the Soviets withdrew their occupation forces quite tardily but without incident. The only geographically weak link on Russia's western frontier is the Polish boundary. The Minindel, however, has partially remedied this situation by creating a Polish Government subservient to the Soviet will. In place of natural defensive barriers, Russia has achieved defense in

---

[10] Koenigsberg, it will be recalled, is a thoroughly German city in which the first Prussian kings were crowned.

depth. The actual frontier is an ethnographic one of very doubtful value, but at the same time the land conveys to Soviet Russia control of the approaches north and south of the Pripet Marshes. To the south of Poland are the Carpathian Mountains which continue from Czechoslovakia almost to the Black Sea. In this region, too, the Soviet Union is buffered by its satellites—Czechoslovakia, Hungary, Rumania, and Bulgaria—all of whom are offensively valuable as well. In view also of their acquisition of Ruthenia on the Danubian side of the Carpathians, the Soviets apparently subscribe to the theory that a good offense is the best defense.

On Soviet Russia's southern frontier, from west to east, are the Black Sea, a mountainous frontier with Iran, a desolate frontier with Afghanistan, Sinkiang, and Mongolia, a river frontier with Manchuria, and finally the Pacific Ocean in the Far East. All in all, the gigantic territory within these borders comprises about one-sixth of the world's land area, and one-tenth of the world's population. In view of this fact and in view of the excellent natural geographic boundaries, it is extremely difficult for non-Soviet observers to understand fully the Soviet desire for additional security.

Another, often overlooked, strategic consideration in Soviet territorial aggrandizement is the position of the USSR as a great naval power. Beginning once again in the north, Russia, in addition to developing a two-months-a-year Arctic sea route from the Atlantic to the Pacific, controls the Barents Sea and the approaches to Spitsbergen. By annexing Petsamo, the USSR has eliminated Finland as a sea power in that area, and has neutralized territory in northern Norway as a threat to Red Fleet control. To the south, the Baltic is close to classification as a Soviet Sea. Although the British Navy controls the North Sea and the entrances to the Baltic, His Majesty's Fleet might experience considerable difficulty if engaged simultaneously by a Soviet Baltic fleet and another Soviet fleet from the ice-free port of Murmansk in the Russian Arctic.

The Black Sea, too, is predominantly a Soviet Sea. Turkey controls the southern shores and the Straits, but is doubtless no match for the Red Fleet in a naval engagement. The Soviet desire here is to alter the Montreux Convention so that no non-Black Sea Power can send its fleet through the Straits, but that Russia can send her fleet in and out in peace and war. It will be recalled in this connection that Soviet naval ambitions have extended into the Mediterranean. The Soviets have made an open request for Tripolitania and a veiled hint for bases on the Dodecanese. They have also received permission to participate in the administration of Tangier at the entrance to the Mediterranean, and have supported the demands of their subsequently recalcitrant satellite Yugoslavia for Trieste in the Adriatic. Moreover, through their Albanian satellite, the Soviets indirectly control a considerable stretch of Adriatic coastline. British concern at this situation is reflected in Foreign Secretary Bevin's remark that Soviet presence in the Mediterranean strikes at the throat of the British lifeline.

In the Far East, the Russian naval position was considerably improved by the approval of two great naval-minded British and American statesmen at Yalta, and by the Sino-Soviet Treaty which inevitably followed. The Soviet Union gained all of Sakhalin Island, and all of the Kuriles to within a few thousand yards of Japan proper. Thus another sea, the Sea of Okhotsk, came under Kremlin control. To the south, the Soviets gained a naval base at ice-free Port Arthur and established themselves quite firmly in the supposedly Free Port of Dairen. With control of Northern Korea, Soviet Russia is now in a strong position in the Yellow Sea in the west, and the Japanese Sea in the east. The Asiatic Fleets of the USSR and the U.S. face each other at this point and in the North Pacific where, historically, Russian Alaska, is but a few miles from Russia itself. On Red Fleet Day immediately following World War II, Stalin announced: "The Soviet peoples wish to see their Navy still stronger and mightier. Our people will create new fighting ships and new bases for the Navy. The task of the Navy is tirelessly to train and improve the cadres of seamen, to master fully the experience gained in the patriotic war, and to raise still higher the naval skill, discipline and organization."[11]

The economic considerations in Soviet territorial aggrandizement appear to have been of secondary importance. Soviet expansion has not been instigated primarily for purposes of economic gain. From all indications, the greatest Kremlin economic interest has been centered in a vast series of intertwining treaties with and between the Soviet satellites in Eastern Europe. These treaties and agreements were established for the purpose of coordinating the economies of the Soviet satellites with that of the socialist motherland. The ostensible idea has been to direct all economy toward reconstruction of the war devastated areas in the Soviet Union, and also eventually to surpass the productive efforts of the capitalist nations. The economies of the satellites have therefore served as supplements of the Soviet economy. Reconstruction

---

[11] For an outstanding analysis on this subject, see Robert J. Kerner, "Russian Naval Aims", *Foreign Affairs,* January 1946.

of the Soviet Union and reconstruction of the satellites will therefore be interrelated.

There are certain theories in the field of political geography that also bear an interesting relation to the concepts of Soviet expansion. For instance, some thoughts of Sir Halford J. Mackinder are especially pertinent. He notes in connection with his Heartland theory ("Who rules East Europe commands the Heartland; Who rules the Heartland commands the World-Island; Who rules the World-Island commands the World") that "it is sufficiently accurate to say that the territory of the USSR is equivalent to the Heartland", except for that area which he refers to as "Lenaland", the northern Asiatic area of great undeveloped natural wealth in the regions of the Lena River.[12] Mackinder further observes that, aside from a very few commodities, the Soviet Union is capable of producing everything it requires. "All things considered," he wrote in 1943, "the conclusion is unavoidable that if the Soviet Union emerges from this war as conqueror of Germany, she must rank as the greatest land Power on the globe. Moreover, she will be the Power in the strategically strongest defensive position." Furthermore, says Mackinder, "The Heartland is the greatest natural fortress on earth. For the first time in history, it is manned by a garrison sufficient both in number and quality."[13]

This theory of Mackinder strikes at the demands of the USSR for additional territory in order to achieve greater security. But the theory simultaneously strengthens the possibility that historical drives in combination with the Communist theory of world revolution will place the Soviet Union within possible realization of the Mackinder thesis: "Who rules the Heartland commands the World-Island; Who rules the World-Island commands the World."

There is another aspect by which the Soviet masks its expansion as the search for security. It is the method of indirect aggression used by the Kremlin in the creation and control of the Eastern European Soviet satellites. A speech by Soviet diplomat Manuilsky on August 22, 1946, perhaps inadvertently revealed the essence of the Communist technique. If the word "reactionary" is replaced by the word "Communist" in his speech, or if it can be assumed that these two words are in fact synonomous, then Manuilsky's statements are very revealing. In regard to the manner in which political-military conflicts are prepared, Manuilsky commented: ". . . we have experience in this respect.

[12] Halford J. Mackinder, *Democratic Ideals and Reality*, (New York, 1942), p. 150. Also "The Round World and the Winning of the Peace", *Foreign Affairs*, July 1943.
[13] Mackinder, "The Round World", *op. cit.*

We also know that such conflicts are usually prepared by terrorist measures within the country preparing them. The first thing is that a reactionary [Communist] government sets out to suppress all opposition amongst its own people by measures of intimidation. Neighborhoods whose population does not approve the government's policy are cordoned off. Military expeditions are sent to towns and villages against malcontent populations. Trade union leaders are arrested and replaced by puppets—often people with a shady past. They then start to exclude from political life not only labor organizations but democratic parties and organizations in general. Democratic leaders are assaulted and assassinated, and the authorities connive with the armed bands which commit these acts. And then the reactionary [Communist] government arranges an election or a referendum to get a free hand for international adventures."[14]

In justification of such indirect aggrandizement, Stalin remarked: "What can be surprising about the fact that the Soviet Union, in a desire to ensure its security for the future, is trying to see to it that governments loyal in their attitude to the Soviet Union should exist in these [bordering] countries.[15] One method by which the Soviet Union sought "to see to it" and "to ensure its security for the future" was to establish common borders for the purpose of effecting control or directly aggrandizing an adjacent state. Russia did just that after the 1939 partition of Poland when a common border was effected with Lithuania. The common border enabled the Soviets to more quickly and easily prepare the way for the 1940 absorption of that country. The 1939 partition of Poland and the acquisition of a part of Eastern Galicia, also established the basis for the 1945 incorporation of Eastern Galicia and thus a common border with Czechoslovakia. The Czechs hardly had time to accustom themselves to their new frontier when the Soviet Government suggested that it would be only right to reunite the Czech autonomous region of Ruthenia to its historic homeland, the Soviet Ukraine. The reunion of Ruthenia, after 800 years of foreign rule, enabled the Soviets to obtain a common border with Hungary and establish a strong measure of control over both the internal and foreign policies of that state and Czechoslovakia. It will be recalled that immediately after the war both of these nations gave indications of functioning as independent sovereign nations, but that situation was relatively short-lived. Hungary succumbed to the Eastern European

---

[14] *Soviet Weekly*, August 29, 1946.
[15] In answer to Churchill's speech at Fulton, Missouri.

version of democracy in May 1947, and Czechoslovakia, much more tragically and shockingly, followed in February 1948.

The Soviet Union also achieved a common border with Norway by the acquisition of Finnish Petsamo in the far north. But the frontier is too short and the area too thinly populated to allow the Soviets to exert much control on Norwegian policy. Nevertheless, the Minindel considers Norway a neighbor nation and would doubtless maintain that it could not help viewing with considerable concern any Norwegian events that might affect the Soviet Union. In the Near East the Soviets remain obviously aware that a successful Kurdistan adventure will establish a common border with Iraq and Syria; and in the Far East they are also aware that their close proximity to Japan might be beneficial if and when the autocratic rule of General MacArthur is replaced by an independent Japanese government. In China, the long common border with Russia has worked to the great disadvantage of the Chinese territorial dominion. Russia has carved out Mongolia, parts of Sinkiang, and has apparently been working toward that same end in Manchuria. Thus there is substantial evidence to show that, with the possible exception of Afghanistan, it is territorially and politically unsafe —or even catastrophic—to be a neighbor of the USSR.

Along the thousands of miles of its Eurasian frontier the Soviet Union has continually applied pressure at widely separate points. The objectives have been so many, so varied and so grandiose that realization of but a small percentage represents a good degree of success. This continual pressure usually has led to an advance in the direction of least resistance. Therefore Central and Eastern Asia must be priority targets in the immediate future. Innumerable facts can be cited to indicate security and expansion are synonomous to the Politburo. It has become increasingly evident that security to the Soviets means domination, aggrandizement, and Sovietization, generally in that order. Stalin's interpretations of Marxism-Leninism have been to the effect that Communism is not secure as long as there remains a single vestige of capitalism. Lenin said, "We cannot live peacefully. Either one side or the other will eventually win out."[16] And Stalin told the American, Harold Stassen: "Lenin is our teacher, and we Soviet people are Lenin's disciples. We never did and never shall go back on Lenin's directives."[17] It would follow that there is certainly no security if there is no peace, and that to "win out" involves a world federation of Soviet Republics. A tenet of Stalinist theory is that whenever possible capitalists will

[16] Lenin, *Works* (Moscow 1924), vol. xxv, p. 505.
[17] *Soviet Weekly,* May 15, 1947.

intervene in a Communist country and restore capitalism—a threat Stalin regards as capitalist encirclement. Furthermore, Communism cannot be finally achieved as long as this danger of intervention and restoration exists.[18] Thus it is that the only security for the Soviet Union lies in aggressive security or expansion. The answer to the often asked question about Soviet policy—where does security stop and expansion begin?—is therefore self-evident.

The constitutional structure of the Soviet Union is also geared to facilitate expansionism. Article 13 of the amended 1936 Soviet Constitution says that the "USSR is a federal state, formed on the basis of the voluntary association of Soviet Socialist Republics. . ." And in Article 2, the political foundation of these republics is stated to be the "Soviets of Working People's Deputies, which grew and attained strength as a result of the overthrow of the landlords and capitalists and the achievement of the dictatorship of the proletariat. . ." Thus it would appear that any former capitalist government that had been overthrown by the proletariat or by an organized segment of the proletariat, and that had in turn established itself as a Soviet Republic, would be eligible for affiliation with the USSR. These provisions of the constitution were used five times to impart a tinge of legality to Soviet aggrandizement during the years of lucrative friendship with Nazi Germany. In quick order through the summer of 1940, Karelo-Finland, Moldavia, Lithuania, Latvia and Estonia became Soviet Socialist Republics.

During this period Soviet Russia desired to legalize its aggrandizement, incorporate border states within the Soviet Union to buffer the Russian heartland, and, in the case of Karelo-Finland and Moldavia, generate a magnet for the attraction of kindred populations not yet within the confines of the USSR.

The creation of these Soviet States before the German attack proved an excellent move. Afterwards the Kremlin maintained that they were independent nations who as members of the Soviet Union had allied themselves with the United Nations in the fight to crush fascism. There was certainly no question of dividing or dismembering the territory of the victorious states of the United Nations, the Soviets indignantly asserted. Thus the USSR Constitution in fact provided the legality of seizure and legitimized Soviet aggrandizement.

During the war it became evident to the USSR that with the formation of a United Nations Organization it would be advisable to have the proletarian dictatorship more adequately represented. It was agreed at Yalta that the Soviet Union should have two additional voices

---

[18] Stalin, *Problems, op. cit.*, p. 25.

in addition to that of Russia in the United Nations Organization. The Kremlin successfully suggested that the voices be those of Byelorussia and the Ukraine in that they both had suffered so much in the war. A year previous to Yalta the Soviet Union—which has always maintained that its Marxist-Leninist foreign policy "foresees developments before they come"—had made changes in the USSR Constitution to meet this very contingency. Article 18 was revised to give each Soviet Republic "the right to enter into direct relations with foreign States, to conclude agreements with them, and exchange diplomatic and consular representatives with them. . ."[19] According to Molotov, the Soviet Republics had "quite a few specific economic and cultural requirements" which could not be covered "in full measure by All-Union representation abroad and also by treaties and agreements of the Union with other States. These national requirements of the Republics," said Molotov, "can be met better by means of direct relations of the Republics with the corresponding States. . . ."[20] Theoretically, this constitutional revision multiplied the voice of the USSR sixteen times and provided fifteen new members to the family of nations. Only two of these nations in addition to Russia actually gained the desired recognition, however, and this was given only for the purpose of assuring Soviet participation in a United Nations Organization. But it was obvious that the Politburo had larger intentions, for in addition to creating Ministries of Foreign Affairs in the Ukraine and Byelorussia, a similar office was immediately established in Armenia and subsequently Lithuania.

The entire procedure is part of the postwar strategy to increase the role of the Soviet Union in world politics. This can not be done by aggrandizement of the 1940 variety. Instead it is now necessary to maintain the legal constitutional structure and outward independence of a Soviet-operated government. In actual fact, the Soviet-dominated countries of Eastern Europe have often been more Communist in character than were the regimes of the Baltic Republics at the time of their absorption in 1940. But these Eastern European and Asian People's Democracies have not become Soviet Republics because they are of greater use to the USSR as seemingly independent nations. It is obviously for this reason that, following the most unanimous plebiscite in history (for independence from China), the Mongolian People's Republic did not then seek admittance to the Soviet Union. On the contrary, the Mongols immediately sought a seat on the Far Eastern Com-

[19] Changes were also made in this connection in Articles 14a, 14g, 60, 77, 78, 83.
[20] Molotov to Tenth Session Supreme Soviet on February 1, 1944.

mission governing Japan, and applied for membership in the United Nations.

Only one incident in postwar Soviet relations has contradicted this trend—the USSR's absorption of the supposedly sovereign republic of Tannu-Tuva, north of Mongolia. With no attempt at the usual legality, this geographically impregnable, mineral-rich, potentially power-producing country was swallowed by the USSR. Subsequently there have appeared in Soviet reports a district referred to as the Tuvian Autonomous Oblast (Region), presumably the former independent state of Tannu-Tuva. The new arrangement, moreover, has placed the Tuvian Oblast directly under the jurisdiction of the Russian Supreme Soviet, unlike other Oblasts which are under a Krai (District).

The same disregard for the usual veneer of legality has also been apparent in the abrogation and abolition of certain autonomous units within the USSR. It is good evidence that the professed regard for the rights of all nationalities—an ideal used to good avail in Soviet expansion—is often ruthlessly violated by the Soviet Union itself. For instance, the German-Volga Autonomous Soviet Republic, which Stalin personally regarded as one of the most advanced national republics of the USSR, was abolished in September 1941 following the disclosure of diversionist activities among its population. Moreover, the action was accompanied by the disappearance of German place-names and their replacement by regular Soviet designations. Two more regions were liquidated in 1943 following the German defeat at Stalingrad: the Kalmyk ASSR south of Stalingrad, and the Karachayev Autonomous Region, a small area at the foot of Mt. Elbrus. The Kalmyk ASSR was divided among surrounding districts and regions, and all local names were changed to Russian. The Karachayev Region suffered a similar fate with half of its territory going to the Russian Soviet Republic and half to the Georgian Soviet Republic. Late in 1943 or early in 1944, the Chechen-Ingush ASSR was also abolished with similar name changes to remove linguistic identity. And in 1945, the Crimean ASSR was abolished and became the Crimean Region of the Russian Soviet Republic. Accompanying name changes eradicated the national identity of the region. Here, as in every case other than the German-Volga ASSR, no reason was given for the Kremlin action.[21]

Despite its various failures in the USSR, the Soviet multinational policy remains one of the strongest agents of expansionism. The Kremlin used to good avail the nationalistic irredentist desires supposedly

21 Theodore Shabad, "Recent Changes in the Political Geography of the Soviet Union," *The American Review on the Soviet Union*, February 1946.

existing among the Ukrainians as justification for the absorption of the Polish Ukraine, Rumanian North Bucovina, parts of Bessarabia, and Czechoslovak Ruthenia. Byelorussian sentiment, although not as vocal as the Ukrainians, provided the justification for the Soviet seizure of Polish areas with Byelorussian population. To the north a comparable technique was employed in the Finnish seizures. And in the south, the Soviet Moldavians suddenly found themselves united with their Rumanian brothers. Along the Turkish frontier, the Armenians and Georgians vociferously demanded return of their alleged historic lands. Since their territorial demands however, overlapped Soviet nationalism was perhaps temporarily out of hand. To the east, the Soviet Azerbaijanis ostensibly lent inspiration to the professed Soviet concern for the welfare of the Iranian Azerbaijanis, a concern which promised to extend the borders of Soviet Azerbaijan at the expense of non-Soviet Iran. On another section of Iran's frontier, the Turkmenians have also expressed an interest in Iranian territory, but as of this writing they remain relatively mild in their territorial demands. Iran's neighbor to the east, Afghanistan, with a population not more than roughly half Afghan, is plagued by the bordering Soviet Republics, which are anxious to become spokesmen for the rights of kindred minorities within Afghanistan. In Sinkiang, the Kazakhs have been instrumental in detaching the racially similar populations of three bordering districts from Chinese control. And the Soviet Turkmenians, although not bordering Chinese territory, have periodically displayed concern over the status of their oppressed brothers in China. Farther east, the Soviet puppet state of Outer Mongolia has been a strong attraction to a great many of the related populations in Inner Mongolia. In China, however, the Soviets have found it unnecessary to rely on any Soviet Chinese. The powerful Chinese Communist Party is an excellent representative.

Thus the Soviet nationalities have been a potent instrument of aggrandizement and influence for the USSR. Furthermore, the USSR has created other related methods to make the Soviet elements of a particular race more attractive to its neglected brethren across the border. Nationalism is befriended and encouraged, and the impression is generated, particularly among the downtrodden nationalities of Asia, that the same national element within the Soviet Union is the official spokesman for all questions relating to that nationality. Apparently the aim of this plan is to attract more and more of these Asiatic nationalities into the USSR, and to undermine Western power or influence in Asia. This scheme has been greatly strengthened by national cultural development in a particular Soviet Republic—for instance, the creation of state libraries to house the national literature, schools instructing in the national language, national theatres, journals, etc.

The Soviet Union also provides some material benefits which are impressive to most of the people of the Asian borderlands. The aura of progress seems to surround especially the great Soviet border cities along the Asian frontier: Batum and Erivan bordering Turkey, Baku and Ashkhabad bordering Iran, Stalinabad bordering Afghanistan, Alma Ata across from the Kazakh area of Chinese Sinkiang, and perhaps Ulan Bator in the Soviet satellite of Outer Mongolia. It is apparent that as long as the USSR presents its program to relatively backward peoples it has an excellent chance of success. It is equally true, however, that the Soviet program will make less progress against a civilization with a strong culture or a nation with considerable material advantages.

As previously pointed out, the great and growing cities of the Soviet borderlands provide an excuse for Soviet expansion, particularly in the direction of small and disorganized border states. Soviet propagandists can always raise the cry of a threat to the motherland's security. Moreover, in the expansion outward from these cities and Soviet nations, the organized units of the Communist Party have found it relatively easy to exploit the wrongs, inequalities, and latent nationalism of their brother nationals within a given bordering state. This fact is particularly true of the Azerbaijanis and Kurds in Iran, and the Kazakhs in Sinkiang, but less true of the Armenians and Georgians in Turkey as that state is in itself relatively strong and backed by the powers of the West.

The instrument by which these wrongs and inequalities are exploited is generally a Communist-front organization, such as the Tudeh and Azerbaijan Democrat Parties in Iran, and is closely akin to the committees of liberation and puppet governments used extensively by the Soviets. The successful use of these instruments, of course, depends to a very great degree on the supporting strength of the Red Army.

In nearly all its methods of aggrandizement, the USSR has sought to establish a basis of legitimacy for its seizures. Negotiations with a Soviet puppet regime help create the illusion of legality although the regime itself may represent an insignificant element of the total population. The same is true of the various front organizations which tend to give the impression of spontaneous popular demand as the basis for legitimizing the often illegal acts of the USSR. The inevitable plebiscite is another technique used to evoke the impression of legitimacy. The

Soviet ballot generally represents a single-party ticket which merely facilitates the process of popular approval. All that is necessary is to establish a compellent for people to vote. The result quite understandably results in an ostensible expression of overwhelming popular support.[22] The same search for legitimacy was evident in the Soviet declaration of war on Japan, and in the continued occupation of Azerbaijan on the basis of the 1921 treaty with Iran.

The Soviet Union has also sought to establish as the legal basis for its postwar territorial demands the idea that changed conditions invalidate existing obligations, as exemplified in the attempted revision of the Montreux Straits Convention and of the Paris Treaty establishing the status of Spitsbergen. A changed state of conditions was also the reason the Soviets advanced for their part in the partition of Poland. The Soviet concept of legality is apparently derived from the premise that time creates legitimacy, or in the words of Montaigne: "Laws take their authority from possession and custom . . . they swell and grow greater as they roll along, just as our rivers do; follow them upward to their sources and you will find them but a bubble of water, scarcely to be seen."

But perhaps most dangerous of all is the strong probability that the Soviet peoples themselves actually consider their Government's aggrandizement and aggression as just and right. They may well be convinced that it is their historic mission to liberate the backward peoples of Asia and the working classes of all countries whom they may honestly regard as enslaved by the capitalist imperialists. Thus the territorial demands of one Soviet people for instance, are justified in the eyes of all Soviet people as acts of liberation and historic reunion. It is a situation fraught with tragedy for in a world of sovereign states and peoples, further Soviet aggrandizement may well result in violent catastrophe for Western Civilization.

[22] This single-party ticket combined with terrorism was also Hitler's method borrowed in fact from the USSR.

BIBLIOGRAPHY

U. S. State Department Documents

Nazi-Soviet Relations 1939-1941, Documents From the Archives of the German Foreign Office, Washington, 1948.

International Conference on Tangier, Final Act of the Conference Concerning the Re-establishment of the International Regime in Tangier, Paris, August 1945 Between U.S.A., U.K., France, U.S.S.R. *Bulletin* XIII, October 21, 1945.

"American Proposal to Withdraw All Foreign Troops From Iran," *Bulletin,* XIII, December 2, 1945.

"Report of Edwin W. Pauley on Industrial Conditions in Manchuria," *Bulletin,* XV, December 22, 1946.

The Problems of the Turkish Straits, Near Eastern Series 5, 1947.

Korea's Independence, Far Eastern Series 18, 1947.

Treaties of Peace With Italy, Rumania, Bulgaria, Hungary, and Finland, 1947.

The Treaty of Brest-Litovsk 1918.

Miscellaneous Documents

United Nations General Assembly. Report of the Security Council Covering the Period July 16, 1946 to July 15, 1947. Document A/366, August 21, 1947.

United Nations Security Council, January 18—March 1, 1946. Official Records, First Year, No. 1, July 10, 1946.

French Ministry of Foreign Affairs, *Les Accords Politique en Europe Orientale* (Notes Documentaires et Etudes, No. 884, April 21, 1948).

British Foreign Office, Armistice with Finland, signed at Moscow, September 19, 1944. London, Cmd. 6586, 1945.

A Colection of Official Documents and Press Extracts on Soviet-Polish Relations, 1944-1946. London, *Soviet News,* 1946.

Soviet Foreign Policy During the Patriotic War, Documents and Materials, translated by Andrew Rothstein. London, 1944, June 22, 1941 to December 31, 1944.

Full texts of the Yalta Agreements and the Potsdam Accords can be found in the *New York Times,* March 25, 1947.

All agreements, armistices, conference proceedings and treaties not specificially mentioned above and relevant to this study may be found in the *New York Times* by consulting the index for the subject and year. Official and semi-official Soviet publications, *Izvestiya, Pravda, Moscow News, Soviet News,* etc., print the texts of treaties and agreements, etc., as well as official statements by Soviet negotiators and diplomats.

GOVERNMENT NEWPAPERS AND PERIODICALS

Department of State, *Bulletin*, Washington, D. C., 1939 ff.; Department of State, *Documents and State Papers*, 1948 ff.; *Izvestiya*, Moscow, 1939 ff.; *Moscow News*, Moscow, April, 1949—June, 1941; *New Times*, Moscow, 1945 ff.; *Pravada*, Moscow, 1939 ff.; *Radio Bulletin*, American Legation, Bern, 1944 ff.

REFERENCE WORKS

Bolshaya Sovetskaya Entsiklopediya, Moscow, 1926-1931, Vol. 1-21.
Bolshaya Sovetskaya Entsiklopediya, Moscow, 1948 (Supplement volume).
Campbell, John C., *The United States in World Affairs*, 1945-1917. Council on Foreign Relations, New York.
Mallory, Walter M. (ed), *Political Handbook of the World*, 1948, 1949, New York.
New International Year Book, 1939-1949, New York.
Year Book of World Affairs, 1947, 1948, London.

NEWSPAPERS

New York Times, 1939 ff.; *The Times*, London, 1939 ff.; *Manchester Guardian*, 1939 ff.; *Washington Post*, 1945 ff.; *New York Herald Tribune*, Paris edition, 1947 ff.; *Soviet War News*, London, February 1942—May 19, 1945; *Soviet News*, London, May 19, 1945 ff.; *Soviet War News Weekly*, London, February 1942—May 24, 1945; *Soviet Weekly*, London, May 24, 1945 ff.; *For a Lasting Peace, For a Peoples Democracy*, Belgrade and Bucharest 1947 ff., issued by the Cominform; *Journal de Geneve*, 1945 ff.; *Baltic Times*, Tallinn, 1939—June 1941; *L'Humanite*, Paris, 1947 ff.; *France-Soir*, Paris, 1947 ff.

PERIODICALS

American Political Science Review, Madison, Wisconsin, 1945 ff.; *American Review on the Soviet Union*, New York, 1939 ff.; *Annals of the American Academy of Political and Social Science*, Philadelphia, 1945 ff.; *Bulletin of International News*, London, 1939-1945; *Contemporary Review*, London, 1939 ff.; *Current Digest of the Soviet Press*, Washington, D. C., 1949 ff.; *Current History*, Philadelphia, 1939 ff.; *Economist*, London, 1939 ff.; *Foreign Affairs*, New York, 1939 ff.; *Foreign Policy Reports*, New York, 1939 ff.; *Fortnightly*, London, 1939 ff.; *Great Britain and the East*, London, 1939 ff.; *International Affairs*, London, 1939 ff.; *Middle East Journal*, Washington, D. C., 1947 ff.; *New Statesman and Nation*, London, 1939 ff.; *Nineteenth Century and After*, London, 1939 ff.; *Observer*, London, 1939 ff.; *Pacific Affairs*, New York, 1939 ff.; *Political Science Quarterly*, New York 1939 ff.; *Politique Etrangere*, Paris, 1939 ff.; *Quarterly Review*, London, 1939 ff.; *Review of Politics*, South Bend, Indiana 1939 ff.; *Slavonic and East European Review*, London, 1939 ff.; *Soviet Press Translation*, Seattle, Washington 1948 ff.; *Spectator*, London 1939 ff.; *World Today*, London 1945 ff.

AUTOBIOGRAPHIES AND BIOGRAPHIES

Byrnes, James F., *Speaking Frankly*, New York 1947.
Churchill, Winston S., *The Second World War*, Vol. 1 and 2, London, 1948-49.

Hull, Cordell, *Memoirs of Cordell Hull*, New York 1948.

Sherwood, Robert E., *Roosevelt and Hopkins*, New York 1948.

ARTICLES AND MONOGRAPHS

Bacon, E., "Soviet Policy in Turkestan" *The Middle East Journal*, Washington, D. C., October 1947.

Ballis, W., "Soviet Russia's Asiatic Frontier Technique" *Pacific Affairs*, New York, March-November 1941.

Beazley, R., "Some Aspects of Soviet Russia's Foreign Policies", *Quarterly Review*, London, October 1944.

Beloff, Max, "No Peace, No War", *Foreign Affairs*, New York, January 1949.

Bienstock, G., "Four Hundred Years of U.S.S.R. Foreign Policy", *Nineteenth Century and After*, June-July 1939.

Bilmanis, Alfred, *Baltic States and World Peace and Security Organization*, Washington, D. C., 1945.

Bowman, Isaiah, "The Strategy of Territorial Decisions", *The Foreign Affairs Reader*, New York 1947.

Bukharin, N., "Imperialism and Communism", *Ibid*.

Castlereagh, Viscount, "Russia's Search for Security", *Fortnightly*, London, September 1946.

Crankshaw, E., "Russia in Europe—The Conflict of Values" *International Affairs*, London, October 1946.

Davidson-Houston, J. V., "Russia in Asia", *Royal Central Asian Journal*, London, July-October, 1946.

Elphinston, W. G., "The Kurdish Question", *International Affairs*, London, January 1946.

"Finnish Peace Settlement with the U.S.S.R.", *Bulletin of International News*, London, March 23, 1940.

Fisher, R. H., "Agreements and Treaties Concluded by the U.S.R.R. in 1945" Department of State *Bulletin* XV, September 1, 1946.

Galin, A., "The Foreign Policy of the U.S.S.R.", *Soviet War News*, November 25, 1944.

George, P., "L'Extreme-Orient Sovietique", *Politique Etrangere*, Paris, July 1946.

Gurian, W. "Permanent Features of Soviet Foreign Policy," *The Year Book of World Affairs*, London, 1947.

Historicus, "Stalin on Revolution", *Foreign Affairs*, New York, January 1949.

Hopper, Bruce C., "Narkomindel and Comintern", *Foreign Affairs*, July 1941.

"Imperial and Soviet Russia in Manchuria," *The World Today*, London, September 11, 1946.

"Studies in the History and Economy of Tuva," by R. Kabo, reviewed by Owen Lattimore, *Pacific Affairs*, New York, December 1937.

Kennedy, A. L., "The Expansion of Russia", *Quarterly Review*, London, January 1947.

Kerner, Robert J., "Russian Naval Aims" *Foreign Affairs*, New York, January 1946.

——————, "Russian Policy in the Far East", *Yale Review*, New Haven, September 1945.

Kolarz, W. J., "Russia and the Middle East", *Fortnightly*, London, June 1947.

Lattimore, Owen, "Outer Mongolia and Urinaghai", *The China Year Book*, Shanghai, 1939.

——————————, "The Outer Mongolian Horizon", *Foreign Affairs*, New York, July 1946.

Lenczowski, George, "The Communist Movement in Iran", *The Middle East Journal*, Washington, D. C., January 1947.

Mackinder, Sir Hartford J., "The Round World and the Winning of the Peace," *Foreign Affairs*, New York, July 1943.

Malakhov, M., "Afghanistan", *New Times*, Moscow, April 1946.

Mandel, William, "The Soviet Far East", *American Review on the Soviet Union*, New York, February-March, 1942.

Mansvetov, Fedor S., "Russia and China in Outer Mongolia," *Foreign Affairs*, October, 1945.

Muller, Edwin, "Behind the Scenes in Azerbaijan", *American Mercury*, New York, June 1946.

Pernot, M., "The Soviet Union and the Mediterranean", *Fortnightly*, London, December, 1945.

Radek, Karl, "The Bases of Soviet Foreign Policy", *The Foreign Affairs Reader*, New York, 1947.

Rondot, P., "L'Union Sovietique et les Confins Irano-Kurdes du Moyen-Orient." *Politique Etrangere*, Paris, October, 1945.

Roosevelt, Jr., Archie, "The Kurdish Republic of Mahabad", *The Middle East Journal*, Washington, D. C., January 1947.

Rubenstein, N., "Soviet Foreign Policy and Its Principles", *New Times*, Moscow, March 17, 1948.

Shabad, Thedore, "Recent Changes in the Political Geography of the Soviet Union", *American Review on the Soviet Union*, February 1946.

Stalin, J. V., "J. V. Stalin on Postwar International Relations", Full text of interviews to Press Conferences and Exchange of Messages, 1946-1947. *Soviet News*, London, 1947.

Strausz-Hupe, R., "The Western Frontiers of Russia", *Review of Politics*, South Bend, Indiana, July 1947.

Taigin, I., "What We Stand For", *Soviet Weekly*, London, June 27, 1946.

"The Soviet Alliance System 1942-1948", *Documents and State Papers*, Washington, D. C., July 1, 1948.

"Through the Tuva People's Republic", *Moscow News*, Moscow, September 1940.

Timasheff, N. S., "The Soviet Union and World Peace", *Review of Politics*, South Bend, Indiana, October 1946.

Westermann, W. L., "Kurdish Independence and Russian Expansion", *Foreign Affairs*, New York, July 1946.

Wheeler-Bennett, J. W., "From Brest-Litovsk to Brest-Litovsk", *Foreign Affairs*, New York, January 1940.

——————————, ————————, *The Treaty of Brest-Litovsk and Germany's Eastern Policy*, Oxford, 1939.

Winterton, Paul, "The Aims of the U.S.S.R. in Europe", *International Affairs*, London, January 1946.

"X", "The Sources of Soviet Conduct", *Foreign Affairs*, New York, July 1947.

BOOKS AND SPECIAL STUDIES

Armstrong, Hamilton Fish, (ed.) *The Foreign Affairs Reader*, New York, 1947.

Bowman, Isaiah, *The New World*, New York 1928.

Bunyan, James and Fisher, H. H., *The Bolshevik Revolution 1917-1918*, Stanford University, California, 1934.

Carr, E. E., *The Soviet Impact on the Western World*, New York, 1947.

Cressey, George B., *Asia's Lands and Peoples*, New York, 1944.

—————————, *The Basis of Soviet Strength*, New York 1945.

Dallin, David J., *Russia and Postwar Europe*, New Haven, 1943.

—————————, *Soviet Russia's Foreign Policy 1939-1942*, New Haven, 1942.

Dennis, A. L. P., *The Foreign Policies of Soviet Russia*, New York, 1924.

Fifield, Russell H. and Pearcy, G. E., *Geopolitics in Principle and Practice*, Boston, 1944.

Fischer, Louis, *The Great Challenge*, London, 1947.

—————————, *The Soviets in World Affairs*, New York 1930.

Gregory, James S., and Shave, D. W., *The U.S.S.R., A Geographical Survey*, London 1947.

Hamzavi, A. H., *Persia and the Powers*, London, 1946.

History of the Communist Party of the Soviet Union, New York, 1939.

Hrdlicka, Ales, *The Races of Russia*, 1919, Washington, D. C.

Hyamson, A. A., *A Dictionary of International Affairs*, Washington, D. C., 1948.

Istoria Vsezoiuznoi Kommunisticheskoi Partii, Moskva, 1938-1945.

Lenin, V. I., *Collected Works*, Moskva, 1924.

—————————, *Selected Works*, London.

Lorimer, Frank, *Population of the Soviet Union, History and Prospects*, 1939, Geneva League of Nations of Nations Economic Financial and Transit Department, 1946.

Mackinder, Sir Halford J., *Democratic Ideals and Reality*, New York, 1942.

Mandel, William, *The Soviet Far East and Central Asia*, New York, 1944.

—————————, *A Guide to the Soviet Union*, New York, 1946.

Martin, John Stuart (ed.), *A Picture History of Russia*, New York 1945.

Moore, Hariet L., *Soviet Far Eastern Policy 1931-1945*, Princeton, 1945.

Nicolson, Harold, *The Congress of Vienna*, London, 1946.

Pares, Sir Bernard, *A History of Russia*, Edition, New York 1947.

Rossi, A., *Deux Ans d'Alliance Germano-Sovietique Août 1939—Juin 1941*, Paris 1949.

Roucek, Joseph S. (Ed.), *Contemporary Europe*, New York, 1947.

—————————, (Ed.), *Governments and Politics Abroad*, New York, 1947.

Schuman, Frederick L., *Soviet Politics at Home and Abroad*, New York 1948.

Somerville, John, *Soviet Philosophy*, New York 1946.

Stalin, J. V., *Problems of Leninism*, Moscow 1931-1947.

Stalin, *Voprosy Leninizma*, 1945.

Timasheff, N. S., *The Great Retreat, The Growth and Decline of Communism in Russia*, New York, 1946.

Treviranus, G. R., *The Russian Revolutions*, New York, 1944.

Vernadsky, George, *A History of Russia*, New Haven, 1943.

Wheeler-Bennett, J. W., *The Forgotten Peace*, New York, 1939.